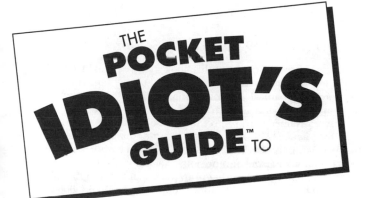

Choosing Wine

by Philip Seldon

alpha
books

International Standard Book Number: 0-02-862016-X
Library of Congress Catalog Card Number: Available upon request.

06   05   04   8   7   6

Interpretation of the printing code: the rightmost number of the first series of numbers is the year of the book's printing; the rightmost number of the second series of numbers is the number of the book's printing. For example, a printing code of 97-1 shows that the first printing of the book occurred in 1997.

Printed in the United States of America

Publisher: Gretchen Henderson
Director of Editorial Services: Brian Phair
Editor: Sora Song
Production Editor: Phil Kitchel
Copy Editor: Cindy Morrow
Illustrator: Judd Winick
Designer: Glenn Larsen
Cover Designer: John Viener
Indexer: Chris Barrick
Production Team: Linda Knose, Daniela Raderstorf, Maureen West

Contents at a Glance

Introduction

Do you find yourself paralyzed when confronted with a wine list? Does a wine store seem like a foreign country altogether? Do you wonder why some wines cost so much more than others? Do you wish you could decipher all those confusing wine labels? If so, this is an essential book for you.

No matter who you are—an ordinary consumer or an experienced gourmet with a fair knowledge of wine—there's something valuable in this book for you. You need practical, down-to-earth information written in plain English... not in the arrogant proclamations found in some other wine books.

I wrote this book for *you*. I've been inside the wineries, the wine cellars, and the warehouses of the distributors and major retailers. I've asked the questions and heard all the answers, some true and others not so true. Over the course of 25 years I've tasted more than 200,000 wines and have seen the improvement in quality and consistency all over the world as modern winemaking technology has replaced antiquated "traditional" winemaking methods. In this little book, I've boiled down everything I learned over the years about tasting wine and choosing the right wine; now you can benefit from my research quickly and easily—even while you're right there in the wine shop.

This book will help you:

➤ Untangle the complicated world of wine.

➤ Find the best wines and the best wine bargains in your local wine store.

➤ Understand and be able to distinguish the different characteristics of fine wine.

➤ Figure out what you can expect from a bottle even before your first taste.

But most important, this book will help you *relax* when you are in a restaurant, a wine store, or with wine-knowledgeable friends who fancy themselves connoisseurs.

Extras

This no-nonsense book will guide you through the complicated process of choosing wine. To make that journey even easier, you'll find helpful boxes throughout the book that provide you with extra information. Here's what each box contains:

Wine Wisdom

These tips will give you insiders' views of the wine world or offer helpful hints on choosing wine (and might even save you money!).

Grape Alert

These boxes will caution you about practices in the wine world that could end up costing you money.

Wine Word

These definitions of wine terms ensure you'll pick up the right lingo, and be able to use it like a true-blue connoisseur.

Trademarks

All terms mentioned in this book that are known to be or are suspected of being trademarks or service marks have been appropriately capitalized. Alpha Books and Penguin Group (USA) Inc. cannot attest to the accuracy of this information. Use of a term in this book should not be regarded as affecting the validity of any trademark or service mark.

Chapter 1

Wine Primer

In This Chapter

➤ How a basic knowledge of wine will make drinking it more enjoyable

➤ What is wine?

➤ The types of wine

➤ The quality categories of wine—from ordinary to works of art

In this chapter you'll learn why wine is more than just an ordinary beverage. Wine is the fermented juice of grapes or other fruit, but in this book we'll be concentrating on grapes. Through a combination of centuries-old tradition and late 20th-century technology, these unassuming-looking fruits can be turned into anything ranging from a simple and enjoyable drink to a complex and noble tribute to the winemaker's art. Wine comes in many types and qualities, and this chapter provides an introduction to the awesome but thoroughly accessible world of wine.

This Book Is About Wine

If you're serious about learning about wine, you probably have a lot of questions. For example, what distinguishes a mediocre wine from a great wine? Try the following analogy:

Have you ever heard Beethoven's Fifth played by a high school orchestra? The orchestra had rehearsed diligently, everyone was in time and on key, and the result was pleasant enough. But if this was your first exposure to Beethoven, you probably wondered why so many generations have been so awed by the scowling, shaggy-haired maestro.

If, on the other hand, you heard the same symphony played by, say, the New York Philharmonic, you would hear what was missing from the high school orchestra's rendition: subtlety, style, and flavor. A great conductor knows just how to highlight the subtle nuances of the music and to bring forth the talents of each musician. Even within the group of world-class orchestras, each has its own unique style, which further sets it apart from the mainstream. The flavor of the individual musicians' performances lies in the rich harmony of sounds, and it makes you want to hear more. Instead of applauding politely, you want to stand up and yell, "Bravo! Bravo!"

Wine Word

These are three keywords to remember when learning about wine: *subtlety*, *style*, and *flavor*.

What Is Wine?

At the most basic level, wine is fermented fruit juice. In simple terms, *fermentation* is the conversion of sugar—in the case of wine, grape sugar—into alcohol by the interaction of yeast. Wine can be made from a number of fruits—from apples to pomegranates. As stated earlier, however, the focus of this book is wine made from grapes.

Three factors interact to determine the character of a wine:

➤ The grape variety and how it's grown

➤ The climate and soil where the grapes are grown

➤ The vintner's (winemaker's) creative or commercial objective and winemaking skills

The vintner has the dual role of scientist and artist. Europeans tend to favor the artistic element, while New World winemakers accent the scientific. Globally, winemakers today have sophisticated technology that enables them to make good quality wine at the lowest price (a good thing to know when you feel like telling off snobbish acquaintances). Technology serves as the background for artistry, enabling winemakers to infuse their wines with the subtle differences in flavor and style that distinguish the products of one vintner from another, grapes and environment being the same.

What Kind of Wine Is My Wine?

Understanding things such as harmony and subtlety are essential to appreciating fine wine, but that understanding doesn't address the practical considerations that separate a superb wine from a merely good one, and a good one from one that is mediocre. For example, why do some German Rieslings stand head and shoulders above those wines made from the same grape variety in California?

Conversely, why does a Napa Valley Cabernet Sauvignon sometimes run circles around an Italian Chianti Classico? European or New World wines are not inherently "better" or "worse" than other wines. A number of factors are involved, and the quality of the end product depends on the interaction between those factors.

To help you understand what to expect from a particular wine, you need to understand what kind of wine you're drinking. In the next sections, I'll cover the basic types of wine: table wine, sparkling wine, fortified wine, and aperitif wine.

Wine Wisdom

The alcohol content of table wines ranges from 9 to 14 percent. Fortified wines—wines with more than 14 percent alcohol—are subject to higher taxation and are, therefore, classified separately from lower alcohol wines.

If Wine Is Not Made out of Wood, Why Do They Call It Table Wine?

If the term *table wine* evokes the image of a bottle or carafe sitting on a red and white checkered tablecloth, you have the right idea. Table wines are reds, whites, and rosés produced to accompany a meal. Most of the wines we drink and will discuss in this book fall into this basic category.

Do Varietal Wines Belong in *Variety* Magazine?

Varietal wines are named for the primary grape used to make the wine. You'll notice that most U.S. wines bear varietal names, such as Chardonnay or Cabernet Sauvignon. Most European wines, however, are named for the wine region—Burgundy or Bordeaux—instead of the grape, but this general rule is starting to change as winemakers capitalize on the powerful marketing tool of varietal names.

Some varietal wines use one grape exclusively, while others blend the dominant grape with other grape types. When different kinds of grapes are blended, the wine must contain—by law—a minimum percentage by volume of the primary grape. There's considerable variance in the regulatory legislation.

For example:

> ➤ In California and Washington, the minimum percentage of the designated grape is 75 percent.

> ➤ In Oregon, it's 90 percent (with the exception of Cabernet, which can be 75 percent, as can its northern and southern neighbors).

> ➤ In Australia and the countries of the European Union, the minimum percentage is 85 percent.

Sparkling Wine—More than Champagne

Sparkling wine is wine with bubbles—like soda but not artificially carbonated. Sparkling wine was first perfected in the Champagne region of France in the Eighteenth Century by Benedictine monk and cellarmaster Dom Perignon. Upon seeing the bubbles in his glass, the good brother eloquently captured the essence of his discovery with the words, "I am drinking stars."

In the United States, the terms *champagne* (remember that lowercase *c*) and *sparkling wine* are often used synonymously. Legally, winemakers in the United States, Canada, and Australia are allowed to use the appellation *champagne* for their sparkling wines on one condition: The bubbles must be produced naturally during the fermentation process and not added through artificial carbonation. Otherwise, the wine-making method and the choice of grape are up to the producer.

In France, home of the Champagne region, the story is entirely different. Understandably, the French would not be satisfied to use the name of their fine and cherished creation for any old generic effervescent wine—as *Coke* is used for *cola*. In France, only sparkling wines made from grapes grown in the Champagne region may bear the name Champagne, and the same is true for all European Union nations. The New World, as usual, makes up its own rules.

Wine Wisdom

Personally, I don't approve of the way the Champagne name has been co-opted for generic usage. When buying domestic sparkling wines, remember that those labeled *sparkling wine* are of a superior quality to those labeled *champagne*. Resist the temptation to go for the champagne name at a cheap price.

Fortified Wines—Strong and Powerful

Fortified wines are wines whose alcohol content has been increased by the addition of brandy or neutral spirits. They usually range from 17 to 21 percent alcohol by volume. Ports, sherries, Marsalas, and Madeiras are all fortified wines. In the United States, they are often regarded as an acquired taste. Dessert wines are almost always fortified wines. Most, but not all, dessert wines are sweet; they are best suited to drinking alone or after a meal. The terms *fortified wine* and *dessert wine* are often used interchangeably.

Aperitif Wines—Great for Cocktail Hour

Technically, aperitif wines are white or red wines flavored with herbs and spices to give them a unique flavor (and often, a unique color). Vermouth falls into this category. Lillet, which is a lot more popular in Europe than in the States, is another example.

What Color Is My Wine?

The three basic colors of wine are white, red, and pink. Within each color category, there are a variety of gradations, which can sometimes provide clues to the wine's taste quality (such as lightness, fullness, clarity, brilliance) and age. More importantly, the appearance of the wine can reveal flaws, so you should take note of these before your initial tasting sip. Because a wine's color can offer clues to the wine's quality, you should drink wine from clear glasses.

If White Wine Isn't White, Why Don't They Call It Yellow?

White wine essentially means that the wine lacks red pigment. If wine shops had swatch books for customers as do paint emporiums, white wines would cover a spectrum from pale straw to light green-yellow, and from yellow to deep gold.

White wine attains its color—or lack of color, depending on your perspective—in one of two ways. Most frequently, it's made from white grapes. (Of course, white grapes are actually green or yellow or a combination of the two.) White wine can also be made from red grapes. Because the red pigment comes from the skin, not the juice, of red grapes, the juice of any variety of grape can be fermented without the skin, and the resulting wine will remain white.

Red Wine Is Sometimes Red

Red wine is easily identified by its deep red color. In the swatch book, red wines would cover the spectrum from pale brick to deep ruby, from purple to almost inky. In winemaker's language, the red wine is made from black grapes (although I'll continue to refer to them as red). During the fermentation process, the skins are left in contact with the colorless juice, and...voilà!...red wine.

Wine Word

Tannin is an astringent acid derived from the skins, seeds, and stems of grapes, and even from the wooden casks in which wines are aged.

The Tannins Pucker in Red Wine

The skins of red grapes also contain *tannin*, which is the key to the major taste distinction between red and white wines. The longer the juice is left in contact with the skins and wooden casks, the higher the tannin content of the wine. If you're not used to the taste of a strong red wine, you may find yourself puckering up. You may have had a similar sensation the first time you tasted strong tea (which, like wine, contains tannic acid) or lemonade (which contains citric acid). After you're used to the taste of tannin, you'll miss it when it's not there.

In wine language, tannins produce the firmness of a red wine. A wine with a high tannin content may taste bitter to even the most seasoned wine lover. This is one reason that red wines are matched carefully with a meal. A wine that tastes unpleasantly bitter on its own may be the perfect complement to a steak or roast beef dinner.

A Rosé Is a Rosé Is a Rosé...

The third shade (type) of wine is recognized by its pink color—and no, it's not made by mixing red and white wines together. Rosé wines are made from red grapes; the juice is left in contact with the skins for only a few hours—just long enough for the wine to absorb a tinge of color and very little tannin. Technically, what are now called *blush* wines are lighter than rosé wines.

What Quality Wine?

Wine comes in several qualities, but the wine industry and many authors differentiate only two categories: everyday or jug wine and premium wine, with the premium category encompassing wines that sell anywhere from about seven dollars per bottle to several hundred dollars per bottle. Clearly, this premium category lumps most wines into one group, and doesn't do much to distinguish among them.

To better explain wine quality, then, I divided the premium category into three subcategories: simple premium (which, of course, are distinct from simple wines), mid-premium, and super-premium. I've also added a new category—noble wines—for those rare wines that evolve into magnificent works of art when fully matured. The industry term *fine wine* describes wines that are bottled in glass (not in plastic bottles or boxes) and closed with a cork (as opposed to a screw cap). But now that many everyday wines sport corks rather than screw caps, I'll use this term to refer to wines that are in the mid-premium quality category or better.

Jug Wines and Everyday Wines—For When You're on the Cheap

What does the term "jug wine" invoke? A dorm party still raging after you kicked the keg? A group of burly, jeans-clad, baseball-capped, just-barely-old-enough-to-drink rugby players slamming a big ol' jug on the frathouse floor?

Wine Word

A *jug wine* is an inexpensive wine sold in a large bottle. Generally, they sell for less than six or seven dollars per bottle and are suitable for everyday drinking.

Actually, jug wines don't always come in jugs. Many now come in magnums. Over the years, they've gotten a lot of bad press. Jug wines are simple wines made for immediate consumption. They're not really bad, just ordinary. Like the high school orchestra playing Beethoven, it's still Beethoven. You just can't look for a lot of complexity or finesse.

Good jug and everyday wines can be tasty, pleasant, and refreshing. They offer vinous (grape-like) flavor, along with body, balance, and straightforward appeal.

Wine Word

A *magnum* is a wine bottle that contains two regular-sized bottles of wine—1.5 liters total.

Premium Wines—Good Value for Every Day

Premium wines have more character and finesse than jug or everyday wines. They have texture and complexity, and they evoke the flavors and aromas of the grape variety (or varieties) of the region of origin. Unlike jug wines, which have a short aftertaste, the taste of premium wines lingers on the palate, which adds another dimension to the wine-tasting experience; new flavors frequently appear in the aftertaste. Premium wines span the price range from $7 to $35 per bottle, with a similar range in quality. I will use the term "super-premium" frequently in this book to describe the higher end of the premium category with the hope that the wine industry adopts it. It should; the term well describes wines that are close to, but aren't quite, of noble quality.

Grape Alert

Premium wines are a varied lot. As you go up the ladder, each one gains in style and finesse. Simple premium wines have more personality than jug wines, mid-premiums more than simple premiums, and so on. Just because a producer labels his wine a "premium wine" doesn't necessarily mean that you're getting something much better than a jug wine; price isn't always an accurate guide.

Noble Wines—Once You Make the Million-Dollar Deal

In my scheme of wine-quality categories, noble wines are the best of the best fine wines. To simply call them "fine wines" would be like calling Japan's prized Kobi beef "prime cut" or a thoroughbred racehorse a "decent runner." The producers of noble wines spare no expense or effort in the production process, and the result is a wine of breathtaking beauty. These wines have distinctive characteristics that set them apart from all other libations; "breeding" is a good word to describe them, and it's not meant for snob appeal.

Noble wines are like a symphony in perfect harmony, with every note and orchestral nuance clearly discernible. Their unique qualities are enhanced with prolonged aging, so these are the wines you'll see cloistered in climate-controlled cellars. As they mature, they become more and more complex, which is how you end up with a wine that is "delicate, yet assertive." Noble wines are multifaceted, like diamonds. In the world of wine, these wines are true works of art.

What Is "Estate-Bottling"?

An *estate* is a wine plantation where the grapes are grown, fermented, and ultimately bottled. The winery controlling the vineyards is responsible for the whole deal, from the raw materials through the end product. This all-in-one approach to winemaking is a good way to ensure quality. No part of the winemaking operation is farmed out to someone who might give it less than an all-out effort. Because there are no gaps in the chain of accountability, winemakers who take pride in their operation can successfully produce wines that meet their customers' and their own high standards. Most estate-bottled wines are labeled as such.

Grape Alert

A winery that makes jug-quality or inexpensive wines and controls all its facilities and the wine-making process can legally call its wines estate-bottled. Still, that kind of estate-bottled wine remains a simple wine. Just remember that the term *estate-bottled* frequently—but not always—signifies a quality wine.

Why Does Wine Come in Vintages?

The structure of a high quality-wine often depends on its vintage: A famous wine property could produce one-dimensional wines in a poor vintage and glorious, multi-faceted wines in a superb vintage. For that reason it is important to know which vintage the wine came from. We've all seen it in the movies. One way to show that the hero or heroine is elegant and sophisticated, the party is chic, or the occasion momentous, is to have someone hold up a bottle announcing, "Lafite '61." Or '45 or '72 or '59.

The truth is, we've all been sold a bill of goods. American consumers have been led to believe the myth that a vintage date means quality, and that only inferior or inexpensive wines are not "vintaged"; merchants, then, are now able to sell mediocre wines at excessive prices. In reality, a vintage date on a bottle often has very little bearing on the quality of its contents—except with high-quality wines. To be a savvy wine buyer, then, you should understand just what a vintage date on a wine signifies and what it is that makes a good vintage.

Wine Wisdom

Charts are available that rate the vintage years for quality wines. Remember that for most wines below the super-premium level, freshness—not age—is the key to optimum flavor. My vintage chart is on the tearout card in the front of this book.

A vintage date declares when the wine was made, but not how or under what conditions. In short, if you're not familiar with the reputation of an individual producer or vintage, all the label reveals is the wine's age or freshness. Most wines—probably at least 80 percent—do not improve with "cellaring" (prolonged aging). They were meant to be enjoyed two to three years after the vintage date.

Chapter 2

In Terms of Wine

In This Chapter

➤ Wine terms to describe your taste sensation

➤ The role of oak in fine wine

➤ The complex flavors of wine

➤ Aroma, taste, and finish

Ever look at a wine-taster's notes? "Subtle yet assertive, with just a hint of violets and a trace of truffles." Oh yes, and maybe "a touch of tar." Sounds pretty neat, doesn't it? Being able to say something that sounds like nonsense to most people and be hailed as an expert. Of course, tasting being a subjective experience, you might look at the notes of another taster and wonder if the two tasters were drinking the same wine.

Wine tasting is one area where purple prose is accepted, if not encouraged. Wines have the scents of flowers, herbs, fruits, and a host of other evocative elements. They're described as robust or flabby, silky or coarse, with a fleeting or lingering finish. Not only can you expand your sensory experience and awareness, but you can also expand your vocabulary. No longer will you think that "astringent" refers only to your mouthwash or facial cleanser.

Sounding like a Pro

You'll probably notice certain words cropping up repeatedly. *Complex*, for example. Or *acidic*. Or *herbaceous*. Just as English, French, Italian, and German (four languages that are helpful for deciphering wine labels) have their nouns, verbs, and adjectives, wine jargon has its categories for classification. The three adjectives at the beginning of this paragraph all fit into the categories of wine-tasting.

The possibilities are vast, but not unlimited. An over-enthusiastic wine writer might say, "This wine has a triangular structure with a diminished fifth harmony, an elliptical balance, and a nose reminiscent of wild mushrooms, rose hips, and comfrey, with just a *soupçon* of mustard. And a brief but resolute aftertaste." Only he will understand what he means.

You can be creative, but try to stick with the terms you see in this book and in the wine magazines and newsletters. Overall, it's better to learn the real stuff than make up your own vocabulary. Try to evoke comparisons with scents and flavors that you already know such as violets, truffles, chocolate, berries of all sorts, and the like. Of course, it is perfectly acceptable to say that a wine tastes like a Bordeaux, a Cabernet Sauvignon, or a Chardonnay, as this communicates an identifiable style and taste.

Oaky Makes the Wine

In wine jargon, the term "oaky" makes no reference to a song by Merle Haggard or a novel by John Steinbeck. A wine is described as "oaky" if it has received oak flavors from being in contact with oak. The wine will have a woody/oaky scent and taste. These days, oaky wines are very much in favor. Chardonnay, for example, is at the peak of popularity while the non-oaked Riesling is considered by some to be slightly outré. (Remember that taste in wine is purely subjective; there's no reason you can't prefer a non-oaky wine.)

Oak barrels are typically 60-gallon containers (although exact size may vary) that house the wine during one or both stages of vinification. The most expensive wines reach maturity in brand-new barrels with full-power oakiness. (Barrels lose some of their oakiness over time.) Contact with oak imparts special flavor and aroma to the wine. Oaking also acts as a catalyst for chemical changes in the wine, although most winelovers would consider this secondary (or tertiary) to the distinctive quality of an oaked wine.

Wine Wisdom

The *vinification* (wine-making) process is usually divided into two parts. The first is *fermentation*, when the grape juice becomes wine. The second is *maturation* or *finishing*, the period when the newly fermented wine hones its rough edges and goes from callow adolescent to mature adult. Some wines are fermented and finished in oak barrels, while others are oaked only during maturation.

Some lesser wines are made by immersing the maturing liquid in oak chips or oak shavings or even by the addition of liquid essence of oak (illegal in some places; legal in others). The best wines, however, are allowed to sleep happily in those oak barrels.

The term *barrel-fermented* refers to those white wines that went into barrels (usually oak) as grape juice and emerged as vino. The term *barrel-aged* refers to wine put in barrels after fermentation. Red wines are fermented with the grape skins intact in stainless steel containers or large wooden vats. After fermentation, the skins are removed from the liquid and the wines are aged in small oak barrels. Some fruity wines (red or white) are not aged in oak at all.

Brix Are Not Bricks

Brix refers to a measure of potential alcohol based on the sugar content of the grape. The more sugar, the higher the potential level of alcohol. You will frequently see this term on the back labels of wines (California wines in particular) and in wine literature.

Vanilla

No, this is not part of a recipe for cake or cookies. Actually, "vanilla" goes hand in hand with "oaky." New oak barrels contain vanillin, and the wines aged in these barrels take on vanilla flavor as part of their oaky charm. As an ice cream flavor, vanilla may be simple; in a wine, it adds complexity and smoothness.

Winetasters and Other Vinous Terms

You will find many wine terms in advanced wine books, in wine magazines and newsletters, and throughout this book. Here are a few of them to get you up to speed.

Bouquet

Bouquet is the smell of a wine after it has lost its grapy fragrances (something like losing baby fat). The bouquet usually develops after years of aging and continues as the wine matures in the bottle. The result is a complex mix of nuances of flavor that did not previously exist. Sniffing the bouquet of a perfectly aged wine is very much like smelling an arrangement of many different flowers.

Wine Word

The scent of a wine is referred to as its *nose*. *Aroma* describes the scent of a young, undeveloped wine. For an older, more complex wine, the term is *bouquet*. The nose of a wine can be "nonexistent," "weak," "moderate," or "intense." A "closed-in" nose is weak because it has not had the chance to develop.

Finish

The *finish* is the taste a wine leaves after it has been swallowed. In essence, the quality of the wine determines the finish. Simple wines have a short finish or no finish at all. Premium wines generally have a finish that lingers on the palate for several seconds or more and mirrors the taste of the wine. With noble wines, the finish can linger on the palate and go through a kaleidoscope of flavors. This kind of sensory experience is what makes wine appreciation so fascinating.

Aged

An *aged* wine has had a chance to mature in the bottle for several years and acquire complex scents and flavors different from what it displayed in its youth. A wine that has aged to maturity is said to be at its peak. In contrast, a wine that has become tired or lost its flavors from being aged too long is said to be over-the-hill. Something like people.

Bottle Sick

After a wine is bottled, it suffers from the shock of the process. For a period of several months or years, it may be lacking in aroma and taste. When this occurs, the wine is described as being *bottle sick*. It usually recovers after a few months.

Cru Classé

You'll frequently find this term on French wine bottles and in wine literature. It refers to the classification system in which French wines are specifically defined by French wine law. I discuss this concept at great length in the chapters on Bordeaux and Burgundy.

Elegance

Like people, some wines show *elegance* and others do not—similar to being well dressed and perfectly coiffed. An elegant wine provides a sense of grace, harmony, delicate balance, and beauty. It is a characteristic that is found only in the finest of wines.

Éleveur

You will find this French term or its equivalent in other languages on wine labels. It refers to a wine company that buys finished wines and cares for them in its barrel-aging and refining procedures. Often, this firm is also a wine distributor or shipper.

Négociant

This is another French term you will find on wine labels. It refers to the wine broker or shipper responsible for the wine. Some *négociants* buy bottled wines from the wine producers and others buy finished wine and produce blends under their own name. A number of these firms have acquired a reputation for fine wines; their names are worth looking for.

Extract

Extract refers to the non-sugar solids in a wine that are frequently dissolved in alcohol. A wine with a lot of extract will feel fuller on the palate.

Goût de Terroir

No, this does not relate to Ivan the Terrible. This French term is hard to define, but translates into the flavor that comes from the specific vineyard or wine area encompassing the soil, microclimate, drainage, and other characteristics of the vineyard.

Herbaceous

You will find this wine-tasting term used frequently in wine-tasting notes. It refers to an aroma and flavor evocative of herbs, which are frequently found in wines made from Cabernet Sauvignon, Sauvignon Blanc, or Pinot Noir. This characteristic is sometimes desirable and sometimes not.

Legs

No, we're not referring to Marlene Dietrich. The legs of a wine are the "tears" or streams of wine that cling to the glass after a wine is swirled. It is a result of the differences of evaporation rates of alcohol and other liquids, such as glycerin, in the wine. It is usually a sign of a wine with body and quality and is something wine lovers look for. Besides being a sign of a good wine, they are pretty to look at as they develop, stream down the side of the glass, and then disappear.

Wine Wisdom

Swirl your wine and take your time sniffing and savoring its lovely scents and nuances. Swirling vaporizes the wine and brings its aromas to the surface of the wine. Think of swirling and sniffing as one continuous motion; give the glass a few swirls, and then bring it right to your nose.

Maître de Chai
A wine cellar in France is called a *chai* and the cellarmaster is called the *Maître de Chai*. He is responsible for tending the maturing casks of wine. Frequently, he is also the winemaker. This is the position of highest importance in a French winery.

Mis en Bouteilles Sur Lie
The French term *Mis en Bouteilles sur lie* indicates wines that were bottled off the lees (sediment) directly from the barrel without racking. Wine bottled this way retains a fresh, lively, zany quality, often with a slight effervescence (prickly sensation) due to the carbon dioxide absorbed during fermentation that did not have the time to dissipate before being bottled.

Middle Body
You will find this term in wine writers' tasting notes, which are frequently published in wine magazines and newsletters. *Middle body* refers to that part of the taste sensation that is experienced after the initial taste impact on the palate. It provides the core of the taste on which assessments are usually based. In a well-structured wine, the first taste ("entry") and the last taste ("finish") should be in harmony with the middle body.

Round
Round is a wine-tasting term that describes the smooth, gentle feel of a wine with a particular alcohol/acid balance that smoothes the sharpness of the acidity and makes a wine feel "round" in the mouth rather than "sharp-cornered."

Unresolved
No, this is not a confused wine. It refers to the impression of a wine that has not yet harmonized its various components in order to create a smooth or harmonious impression—a result of aging.

Charm

Like people, a wine can display charm. Wines that have a lovely scent and taste and are generous with their attributes are frequently described as having "charm." This characteristic transcends quality categories, and it is frequently found in young and fruity wines like those from Beaujolais or Provence.

Off-Dry

A wine that contains a slight amount of residual sugar—from one-half to two percent—is said to be *off-dry*. When the residual sugar is low, it tempers the acidity of the wine and gives the impression of a wine that is softer and easier to drink. At the higher end, the wine is slightly and pleasingly sweet.

Blind Tasting

No, this is not a tasting where you are blindfolded when you taste the wine. It is the practice of hiding the identity of the wine from the wine taster so that his impression will not be influenced by the name on the label. You can do this by placing the open bottles of wine in brown bags when conducting a wine tasting. It's fun to do this at home, but it is *de rigueur* at wine judgings and wine competitions worldwide. (Wine judges do not want to rate a famous wine with a low score lest it be a reflection on their tasting ability.) Some experienced professional tasters in the wine trade correctly point out that they do not need to taste blind when they have confidence in their palate; frequently, famous wines are flawed or not up to snuff in a particular vintage, and it's up to these professionals to determine this so that these wines do not reach the marketplace.

Body

The *body* is the fullness (or lack thereof) that you feel when you roll the wine over your tongue and palate. Body is the product of the wine's alcohol, glycerin, and extract.

It is either light, moderate, or full, and may or may not be in balance with the flavor and other constituents.

Viscosity

No, we are not talking about motor oil. A wine characterized by *viscosity* is thicker, fuller, and has a heavier body than the average wine. The term to use for a full-bodied wine high in alcohol and glycerin, and with more flavor than acidity is "fat." A wine with viscosity will frequently display "legs."

Acidity

Acidity refers to the non-volatile acids in wine, which are principally tartaric, malic, and citric acids. These acids provide the wine with a sense of freshness and (one hopes) balance.

Sufficient acidity gives a wine firm body, while lack of acidity may make it feel "flabby." (And no, despite what you might wish, drinking acidic wines will not provide firmness for flabby thighs and abdomens.)

Wine Word

A wine is said to be *harmonious* if all its elements are in proper relation to each other. The acidity does not overpower the flavor. The body seems right for the other elements of the wine. The aftertaste does not fall short.

Harmony

Harmony refers to the interplay of the wine's constituents. Harmony means smooth, flowing, and compatible. When everything is in sync, the result is a balanced wine.

Balance

Balance refers to the proportion of the various elements of a wine in relation to one another. For example, acid against sweetness, fruit flavors against wood, and tannic alcohol against acid and flavor.

When all the components are working together, like the instruments in a world-class orchestra, the wine is balanced. *Harmonious* is the prime adjective of choice. When wines are imbalanced, they may be acetic, cloying, flat, flabby, or even awkward.

Mouthfeel

While the body of the wine refers to its weight or viscosity, the *mouthfeel* of the wine refers to its texture. Never neglect to savor the wine fully, rolling it in your mouth. And if the tasting environment permits, don't forget your gurgling. The texture and feel of the wine in the mouth is part of the beauty that makes wine so exciting. Overall, the adjectives used to describe mouthfeel are tactile (the same ones you use to describe textures): silky, velvety, rough, coarse, or smooth. The one descriptive term that doesn't adhere to this rule is the "pucker" of tannic red wines. The puckering quality may seem strange at first, but as your wine-tasting experience progresses, certain wines will seem flat or dull without it.

Backbone

Backbone refers to the structural framework of the wine, built on the wine's alcohol, acids, and tannins. Think of a wine with backbone the way you'd think of a person "with backbone." A wine with a firm backbone will seem well-structured, and will provide a pleasing mouthfeel. A wine that is flabby will seem to be lacking in acidity, tannins, or flavor.

Finesse and Breed

These are two descriptors that speak for themselves, like Katherine Hepburn and Cary Grant emanating from your wine cellar. If you can't think of a contemporary star who measures up, don't worry about it. Wines with breed and finesse are the loveliest, most harmonious, and most refined wines. The classics. These are the wines that age gracefully and wondrously. Finesse and breed are not usually the qualities of mid-premium or lesser wines. Wines with breed and finesse are those rare noble wines in which all elements of structure, flavor, and complexity combine to a peak of almost indescribable perfection. For these noble beauties, fermentation is merely the beginning of a long life that culminates in a wine comparable to the finest work of art.

Wine Words

When all the elements of structure, flavor, and complexity attain a perfect harmony—sometimes virtually indescribable—the result is *breed* or *finesse*. These terms are frequently used to describe classic noble wines.

It's hard to speak of finesse and breed without throwing in at least a touch of romanticism. Technically, *finesse* is the quality of elegance that separates a fine wine from one that is simply good. Breed goes up even higher. *Breed* is the term we use to describe wines that achieve "classical proportions." It is star quality at its utmost. The quality is usually elusive to describe, but you'll know it the moment you experience it. Noble wines such as Château Lafite-Rothschild, Château Y'quem, or the legendary Burgundy, La Tâche, have finesse and breed.

Grape Expectations

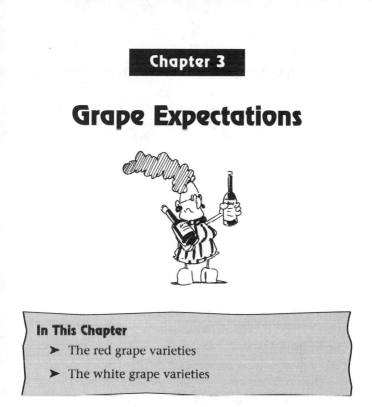

Of a total of about 8,000 grape varieties, only a select few are now on display at your local wine shop. That's good, because it gives you fewer wine names to memorize. But don't get too complacent; there are still many grape varieties to consider. Although many of these grapes first became famous by turning up in the right place—that is, in a famous wine named after a wine place, such as Corton-Charlemagne—they continued in popularity in their own right, and appear on wine bottles named as varietal wines. White grapes are listed here first, then reds. It's not an order of rank or preference, just a convenience.

The Most Popular White Grape Varieties

Most white wines are made from white grapes. Hundreds of white grape varieties are made into wine, but only a handful are seen on wine labels as varietal wines. This section reviews some of the most popular.

Wine Word

The grape variety is technically known as a *cultivar*. You'll see this term frequently in wine literature. It's a fancy name referring to a specific vine variety or clone. A *clone* is a grapevine that has been produced by grafting to retain the genetic characteristics of the mother vine.

Chardonnay

Chardonnay is the *haute* varietal of the white wine grapes. It is known as the king of white grape varieties. Power and finesse are two qualities of this white vinifera, which yields the world's finest white wines.

It's impossible to discuss Chardonnay without mentioning oak. Most Chardonnay receives a restful yet invigorating treatment in an oak bath. The best Chardonnays get their spa treatment inside the traditional French oak barrel, while less expensive wines have to be content soaking in oak chips or in liquid essence of oak.

The flavors imparted by oak have a vanilla, smoky, spicy, or nutty character. These flavors are easy to associate with oak: They're all woodsy qualities. The Chardonnay flavors and scents are rich and fruity. You can name any fruit you like, from apples to mangoes, and chances are you'll taste at least a hint of it in a cool glass of Chardonnay.

The Chardonnay grape grows successfully in many different countries but is synonymous with the celebrated white wines from France's Côte d'Or region of Burgundy. There, it's identified with such legendary names as Montrachet, Meursault, and Corton-Charlemagne. If these sound to you now like the sites of ancient battles, they'll become more familiar as your wine knowledge grows.

Pinot Grigio (Pinot Gris)

Pinot Grigio, or Pinot Gris, is a white vinifera, related to the Pinot Noir. It's known as the Tokay in Alsace, and the Rulander in Germany.

Northeastern Italy is the primary stomping ground for this grape. It's grown in small quantities in the United States, mainly in Oregon, although it's becoming more popular in California.

Sauvignon Blanc

Sauvignon Blanc is an adaptive white vinifera. It's a fairly productive grape that ripens in mid-season. Harvested at full maturity, it offers wines with a characteristic herbaceous, sometimes peppery, aroma. Picked early, the grape is intensely grassy (and yes, that can be a compliment, although it isn't always).

Sauvignon Blanc is higher in acidity than Chardonnay. Some wine lovers savor its crispness; others prefer Chardonnay. Sauvignon Blanc wines are light- to medium-bodied and generally dry. The European varieties are largely not oaked, while the California versions usually are. Maybe Californians just like to experiment. California Sauvignon Blancs range from dry to slightly sweet. "Fumé Blanc" is a popular varietal label.

Riesling

If Chardonnay is the king of white grape varieties, Riesling is its queen. Riesling is a white vinifera variety that gained its ranking among noble grapes through the great Riesling wines of Germany. Unfortunately, the name has suffered a lot of misuse on wine labels. The noble grape is the Johannisberg Riesling; Gray Riesling and Silvaner Riesling wines are actually made from lesser grapes. To add additional insult, vast quantities of simple jug wines from South Africa and Australia are designated as "Rieslings," although they bear little resemblance to the fine wines of the Rhine. Riesling wines frequently taste like peaches or fresh melons.

Grape Alert

Wines labeled *White Riesling* or *Johannisberg Riesling* may be made from the noble grapes of Germany—or they may not. When buying a Riesling wine, be sure to read the label thoroughly and pay careful attention to the fine print to determine which country it was produced in.

Riesling does thrive in a few places outside of Germany, notably Alsace in northeastern France (near Germany), Washington state, and the Finger Lakes district of New York.

Gewürztraminer

Gewürztraminer (ga-VERZ-tra-mee-ner) wines are a lot easier to drink than pronounce. The grape is a clonal selection of the once widely-planted traminer white vinifera. Its name literally means "spicy grape from Traminer."

Gewürztraminer wines have recently gained in stature, due to their distinctive appearance and taste. The wines are deep gold in color, with the spicy aroma of roses and lychee fruit. They're exotic and intriguing. The scent is spicy, floral, and fruity; the flavor is surprisingly dry. The most distinctive examples of Gewürztraminer come from Alsace. U.S. styles tend to be lighter and sweeter than their Alsatian counterparts, but dry Gewürztraminers are also produced in California and Oregon.

Chenin Blanc

This noble white grape originally hails from the Loire Valley in France, where it is used both for still wine and *vin mousseux* (sparkling wines). It's also popular in California, Australia, South Africa, and South America.

Chenin Blanc is a fruity wine ranging from bone dry to slightly and even very sweet. The best sweet versions come from the Côteaux du Layon and Vouvray in France and occasionally rise to legendary quality. Wines of the highest quality have high acidity and an unusual oily texture, aged to a beautiful deep gold color, and can last for 50 years or more. The aroma is typically reminiscent of fresh peaches; when harvested early, the wine is slightly grassy and herbaceous.

The Most Popular Reds

As with white wines, there are hundreds of red wine grape varieties. Similarly, only a handful appear on wine labels as varietal names. The following section will introduce you to the most popular red grape varieties.

Cabernet Sauvignon

Cabernet Sauvignon is the red counterpart to the royal Chardonnay. It's the reigning monarch of the red vinifera. Ideally, Cabernet Sauvignon wines offer great depth of flavor and intensity of color, and they develop finesse and breed with bottle aging.

The red royal grows well in many wine regions, yielding wines that range from outstanding to mediocre in quality. (After all, the grape is not solely responsible for the outcome.) In France, Cabernet Sauvignon takes the credit for the grand reputation of Bordeaux red wines. It's the prime element in many of the finest bottlings. In northern Italy, it can yield reasonable facsimiles of Bordeaux. Cabernet also grows in many eastern European countries, where it is made into pleasant light-style wines.

Cabernet is also an *émigré* that thrives in the California sunshine. Some of its California bottlings are on a par with Bordeaux, and a few attain noble quality. Other California Cabernets run the entire quality spectrum. South American countries, particularly Chile and Argentina, produce Cabernet in vast quantities, but quality can be shaky.

Grape Alert

In the mind of many wine lovers, Cabernet Sauvignon may be synonymous with quality, but things can be different in the real world. The least expensive varieties can lack the firmness of the better quality wines, and the fruitiness may be devoid of the true Cabernet pungency.

Cabernet Sauvignon is a versatile vinifera that works well by itself or in the company of other grapes. It's at its best and longest lived when made with close to 100 percent Cabernet grapes, but it has an affinity for blending with other wines. A few of its favored companions are Cabernet Franc, Merlot, Malbec, and Petit Verdot in the Médoc; Merlot and sometimes Zinfandel in California; and Shiraz in Australia.

Cabernet Sauvignon wines are high in tannin and medium- to full-bodied. Their distinctive varietal character is a spicy, bell-pepper aroma and flavor with high astringency. Deeply colored wines made from very ripe grapes are often minty and cedary, with a black currant or cassis character.

Merlot

This French variety red vinifera is grown in many wine regions. It is an early ripening, medium-colored red grape. As a varietal, it makes wines that are soft and subtle, yet substantial (say that very fast while swooshing the wine in your mouth). The finest Merlots possess great depth, complexity, and longevity.

Merlot has a distinctive herbaceous aroma quite different from the bell pepper quality of the Cabernet. It is softer in tannins and usually lower in acidity, producing a rounder, fatter, and earlier maturing wine.

In the Médoc and other regions of Bordeaux, Merlot is used as an elegant and mellowing component in Cabernet Sauvignon. In the St. Emilion and Pomerol regions of Bordeaux, Merlot is the star, usually comprising 60 to 80 percent of the blend, and producing complex, velvety, and sometimes frightfully expensive wines. In California, Italy, Chile, and elsewhere, an increasing number of wineries are producing varietal Merlots, but primarily using the grape as a blending agent with the more powerful Cabernet. In California terminology, Merlot is the best supporting actor. Cabernet Sauvignon is still the big box office draw.

Pinot Noir

Pinot Noir is one of the noblest of all wine grapes. It is grown throughout the wine world, but success varies due to its sensitivity to soil, climate, and the clonal variant of the vine. This is one temperamental vinifera! Its taste varies with where it is grown; in the Burgundy region of France, it frequently resembles violets and berries.

Wine Wisdom

The very qualities that make Merlot less powerful than Cabernet Sauvignon make it more palatable for some wine drinkers. Don't be intimidated by wine snobs. Merlot is easier to drink by itself and it goes well with lighter foods.

In France, Pinot Noir is the principal red grape of the Côte d'Or region of Burgundy, where it produces some of the world's most celebrated and costly wines. With the exception of Blanc de Blanc, it is used as a base for all Champagnes and is admired for body and elegance.

Zinfandel

Zinfandel is a red vinifera thatis grown commercially only in California—an interesting sort of status. It is related to an Italian grape but, with no French heritage whatsoever, it is exempt from the unfair comparisons many fine California wines have to endure.

The typical character is berrylike—blackberry or raspberry—with a hint of spiciness. Styles vary from light and young to heavy, syrupy, and late harvest.

Even more popular than a full-bodied red Zinfandel in today's market is the blush wine known as white Zinfandel. White Zinfandel endures minimal contact with the grape skins during fermentation; in contrast, Zinfandel reds have a rich, deep color.

Chapter 4

Vive La France!

In This Chapter

➤ Understanding French wine laws

➤ Regions of origin

➤ Are French wines better?

France was a wine country even before Joan of Arc heard her first voice. Records indicate that the Greeks may have introduced wine to Marseilles as early as 600 B.C. Later, the Roman colonization of Gaul resulted in the wide dispersion of vines throughout France—no doubt because wine tasted good, could be kept for a long time, and could be traded easily.

The ancient wines actually bore little resemblance to the wines we enjoy today, but the ever-resourceful French perfected the art of winemaking to produce some of the finest wines on the market. This chapter introduces you to the culture of French winemaking.

Fathoming French Wine Law

The French like to regulate everything, even their chickens—which is good, because France produces the very best chickens. Similarly, the French regulate their wine to the nth degree—all for the better. The French regulations provide the most specific guidelines for interpreting the contents of a wine bottle from its label. In theory, the structure is straightforward and easy to understand. In the real world, however, theory and application do not always match. And when the application is attached to a bottle of one of France's best wines, interpreting the label requires some background knowledge.

What Are Appellations?

The French system of identifying and regulating wine regions is known as the *Appellation Contrôlée* (AOC or AC), translated as "regulated place name." Most French wines are named for places, not grapes. According to French wine law, a wine can aspire to one of four status levels. One of the following French phrases will appear on the label:

➤ **Appellation d'Origine Contrôlée (or AOC)**   The highest tier. On the label, the place name usually substitutes for the "d'Origin." For example: Appellation Bordeaux Contrôlée indicates a wine from the Bordeaux region. These wines range from mid-premium to noble in quality.

➤ **Vin Délimité de Qualité Supérieur (VDQS)**   The second-highest tier, this phrase translates as demarcated wine of superior quality. These wines range from simple premium to premium in quality.

➤ **Vins de Pays**   Literally, country wines. On the label, the phrase is always followed by a place name; it's more of a generic place name, however, generally encompassing a much larger area than the places named in the two higher tiers. These wines resemble the jug and magnum wines you find from California, Chile, and Italy; they are simple-premium wines.

➤ **Vin de Table**   This label indicates ordinary table wines. These wines have neither a region of origin nor a grape variety on the label. You will rarely find a wine of this quality in the United States; these wines are sold in plastic bottles in France. At best, they are jug quality, but sometimes are not even that good.

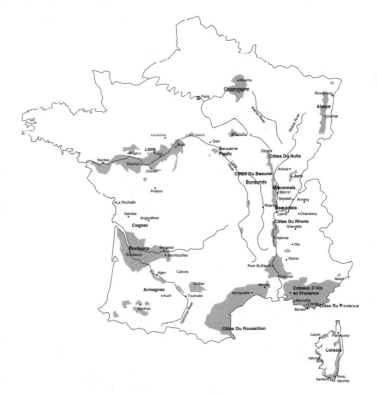

Many French wines are named for the places they come from in France.

Most of the wines in the two lower tiers were not marketed much in the United States until recently; wines labeled *Vins de Pays D'Oc* (and certain other regions), however, have become more and more available as these regions are able to make fine varietal and blended wines that are much better than the Vin de Pays wines traditionally produced.

The first or lowest tier within the AOC category refers to a very broad geographic region whose wines meet certain minimum standards. From here, the regions keep getting tighter and higher in quality. Some outstanding vineyards even have the honor of their own appellation. From the broadest to the most specific, the Appellation Contrôlée name refers to tiers; think of concentric circles with districts within districts:

➤ **First tier** A region (such as Bordeaux or Burgundy). Simple-premium to premium quality. Wines are labeled simply as Bordeaux, Bordeaux Supérieur, and so on.

➤ **Second tier** A district (such as Haut-Médoc or Côte de Beaune). Somewhat higher in quality than the first tier but still range from simple-premium to premium quality with some wines occasionally better. Within this tier are sub-districts within an AOC area that produce somewhat better wines (for example, Côte de Beaune Villages and Beaujolais Villages).

➤ **Third tier** A village or commune (such as Pauillac or Meursault). These wines are considerably better than the previous appellation, depending on the producer. When wines are blended from several vineyards within the commune or district, they are known as *regional* or *village* wines, depending on the custom of the locality. These wines range from mid- to super-premium and noble quality. Within such a district, some wines can be much better than others, and the key is to know the château or vineyard names. In Bordeaux, a number of the commune wines are classified as *growths* or *Cru Classé*, which are immediate indicators of higher (or highest) quality. Some of these wines are equal in rank to the fourth tier.

Wine Word

Cru means *growth* in French. It refers to a particular level of quality. The term cru denotes a wine of high quality. A *Premier Cru Bordeaux* is better than a *Deuxième Cru*. In Burgundy, a *Grand Cru* is better than a Premier Cru.

➤ **Fourth tier** A vineyard (such as Le Montrachet). In Burgundy and (rarely) other districts, a wine of extraordinary distinction and fame is honored with its own appellation. These wines are designated as a Grand Cru and are the equivalent of a First Growth (Premier Cru Classé) of Bordeaux.

Although the French regulations for winemakers are strict and complicated, they do nothing to help you, the consumer, decipher them: The only thing that ends up on the label is the designated appellation. Therefore, judging the quality of the wine by the appellation alone requires doing some homework. Technically, the more specific the appellation, the costlier the contents. This guideline doesn't, however, necessarily mean that the wine will be higher quality; even French regulations have loopholes. Another thing to look for on the label is the word "cru." Within certain appellations, the wines are classified into crus, which have legal standing. The cru is another clue to the quality of the wine.

In short, the French wine label looks fairly simple. Deciphering it for quality and value, however, is a lot harder than it appears at first glance. You need to know your French wines to decipher from the label what's in the bottle.

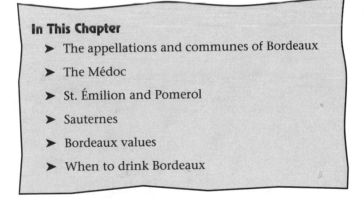

Chapter 5

Bordeaux—
The King of Wine

Sip.

In This Chapter

➤ The appellations and communes of Bordeaux

➤ The Médoc

➤ St. Émilion and Pomerol

➤ Sauternes

➤ Bordeaux values

➤ When to drink Bordeaux

The name *Bordeaux* refers to a large industrial city in the southwest corner of France and the wine regions surrounding it. It is by far the largest quality wine region in the world, and the most prolific producer of famous and high-quality wines. The city of Bordeaux is a major commercial port, and the top wine brokers and shippers maintain their offices along the port's *Quai de Chartrons*.

Bordeaux is the stuff that legends are made of—home of such famous names as Château Lafite-Rothschild, Château Latour, and Châteaux Margaux. Not all of the region's exports are in this rarefied category (fortunately for most of us), and Bordeaux winemakers are also known for producing high-quality, highly enjoyable, and generally affordable wines.

With its appellations, communes, and *crus* (growths), you can easily get a bit lost in Bordeaux. This chapter will unravel the mysteries of the region known for the King of Wine. We'll cover the inner appellations and vineyards that make up Bordeaux, and the different wines, grapes (no, they're not all Cabernet Sauvignon), and price tags.

The wine regions of Bordeaux have districts within districts as the wines get better.

Bordeaux, Vive Bordeaux

Providing the Bordeaux brokers and shippers with their liquid gold are several hundred *châteaux* (vineyards), which produce the outstanding quality wines that have made Bordeaux a legend. A few names—Château Lafite-Rothschild, Château Mouton-Rothschild, Château Latour, and Château Margaux—have become symbols of superlative wine. Names like these have imbued Bordeaux with a sort of *je ne sais quoi* mystique. Before we get carried away, we must note that the region also makes gallons of ordinary wines for local consumption. Because most of these do not appear on our shelves or tables, the legend remains.

Wine Wisdom

Bordeaux produces 10 percent of all French wine and 26 percent of all AOC wine. Most Bordeaux are dry reds. Fifteen percent are dry whites, and two percent are sweet whites, most notably Sauternes. Prices for Bordeaux wines run the gamut: Most fine quality Bordeaux, both red and white, start at about $15 a bottle when they're young. The greatest Bordeaux of extraordinary vintages (which frequently take 20+ years to mature), however, command a king's ransom: Recently a 12-bottle case of 1945 Château Mouton-Rothschild was auctioned for more than $160,000.

Many of the Bordeaux wines you will read about are super-premium and noble quality. They are the wines many winemakers aspire to imitate. When they are young, the typical Bordeaux-classified growth will have a deep ruby hue with aromas of black currants, spice, cedar, fine leather (like fine leather gloves), chocolate, and cassis.

For the first five to 10 years, they can be very vinous and austere with puckering tannins. As they age, their color changes to garnet, frequently with a gemlike brilliance. They are capable of developing an extraordinarily complex bouquet and flavor with more agreeable tannins. On rare occasions, the best will develop an unusual scent that is almost devoid of flavor, like the air after a rainstorm, with subtle nuances of bouquet that are delicate and beautiful. I call this quality "vaporous."

The Médoc Maze

The Médoc is a district—our second tier of wine quality within the larger AOC of Bordeaux. The most famous—and definitely the best—red wine vineyards of the Bordeaux district lie within the Médoc, north of the city along the Gironde River. The best vineyards are situated along a narrow strip of gravelly soil, about 10 miles long and seven miles wide, sometimes less. In this small area, the ideal conditions of climate and soil combine with centuries of winemaking tradition and dedication. Here, the noble Cabernet Sauvignon grape happily thrives.

Wine Wisdom

Under AOC regulations, the region is divided into main regions and subregions. Each subregion or commune defines stricter requirements for soil, winemaking techniques, and, ultimately (and in theory), higher qualities of wine.

The wines of the four major communes of Médoc each have distinct characteristics and subtle nuances, described in Table 5.1, as do the red wines of Graves, a district to the south known for its high-quality wines.

Table 5.1. The Five Major Communes of Médoc and Graves

Commune	Example	Distinct Characteristics
Margaux	Château Lascombes	Moderately tannic; medium-bodied; fragrant, perfumed aromas; complex, generous, and elegant; finesse; long-lived.
St-Julien	Château Léoville-Poyferré	Softer tannins; rich, flavorful; medium/full-bodied; sometimes fruity; elegance and finesse; earlier maturing.
Pauillac	Château Lafite-Rothschild	Firm tannins; rich, powerful, yet with delicate nuances of flavor; firm backbone; full-bodied; extraordinary finesse and elegance (First Growths); black currants and cedar aromas; extremely long-lived.
St-Estèphe	Château Cos d'Estournel	Tannic hard, firm; full-bodied, earthy, and vinous; rarely elegant but pleasingly masculine; slow to mature.
Graves	Château Haut-Brion	Moderately tannic; with (ironically) a gravelly mouthfeel; earthy; early to mature.

The 1855 Classification

If you're still pondering the *Cru* on the label, this should straighten it out. First we go back to 1855, when the organizers of a Paris Exposition asked the Bordeaux Chamber of Commerce to create a classification of Bordeaux wines for the exposition. The Chamber of Commerce delegated the job to the Bordeaux wine brokers, who named 61 superior red wines, dividing them into five categories or crus (the *cru* or *growth* refers to the wine estate) based on price; in those days, price was indeed an indication of quality and fame. While the classification was supposed to be limited to the district of the Médoc, one wine of the Graves, Château Haut-Brion, was also listed because of its excellence and fame.

Wine Words

First Growth is the English translation of Premier Cru—the highest quality level in Bordeaux. A growth is known as a cru in France. In the Médoc, the crus range from First to Fifth growths.

Are you still confused? You're not alone. In general, a cru is a separate classification within an appellation or district in our tier system. Some appellations have classifications, others not so worthy do not. That said, some appellations that are not so worthy have classifications, too. It's very political and confusing. In any event, for the purposes of this chapter, a cru or growth is a classification within a district in Bordeaux. Thus, a classified wine has an appellation *and* a classification designation (or cru), which, in effect, rates all the wines within that particular district.

The listing created by those wine merchants remains today and is still known as the classification of 1855 of the

Médoc. The châteaux listed in Table 5.2 comprise the first and second growths.

Table 5.2. The 1855 Classification of Bordeaux

Château	Commune
FIRST GROWTHS (*Premiers Crus*)	
Château Lafite-Rothschild	Pauillac
Château Latour	Pauillac
Château Margaux	Margaux
Château Mouton-Rothschild	Pauillac
Château Haut-Brion*	Pessac, Graves

* This Graves wine is classified as one of the five First Growths of the Médoc in recognition of outstanding quality.

SECOND GROWTHS (*Deuxièmes Crus*)	
Château Rausan-Ségla	Margaux
Château Rauzan-Gassies	Margaux
Château Léoville-Las Cases	Saint-Julien
Château Léoville-Poyferre	Saint-Julien
Château Léoville-Barton	Saint-Julien
Château Durfort-Vivens	Cantenac-Margaux
Château Lascombes	Margaux
Château Gruaud-Larose	Saint-Julien
Château Brane-Cantenac	Cantenac-Margaux
Château Pichon-Longueville-Baron	Pauillac

continues

Table 5.2. Continued

Château	Commune
Château Pichon-Lalande	Pauillac
Château Ducru-Beaucaillou	Saint-Julien
Château Cos d'Éstournel	Saint-Estèphe
Château Montrose	Saint-Estèphe

THIRD GROWTHS (Troisièmes Crus)

Château	Commune
Château Giscours	Labarde-Margaux
Château Kirwan	Cantenac-Margaux
Château d'Issan	Cantenac-Margaux
Château Lagrange	Saint-Julien
Château Langoa-Barton	Saint-Julien
Château Malescot-Saint-Exupery	Margaux
Château Cantenac-Brown	Cantenac-Margaux
Château Palmer	Cantenac-Margaux
Château La Lagune	Ludon
Château	**Commune**
Château Desmirail	Margaux
Château Calon-Ségur	Saint-Estèphe
Château Ferriere	Margaux
Château Marquis d'Alesme-Becker	Margaux
Château Boyd-Cantenac	Cantenac-Margaux

FOURTH GROWTHS (*Quatrièmes Crus*)

Château Saint-Pierre	Saint-Julien
Château Branaire	Saint-Julien
Château Talbot	Saint-Julien
Château Duhart-Milon-Rothschild	Pauillac
Château Pouget	Cantenac-Margaux
Château La Tour-Carnet	Saint-Laurent
Château Lafon-Rochet	Saint-Estèphe
Château Beychevelle	Saint-Julien
Château Prieure-Lichine	Cantenac-Margaux
Château Marquis-de-Terme	Margaux

FIFTH GROWTHS (*Cinquièmes Crus*)

Château Pontet-Canet	Pauillac
Château Batailley	Pauillac
Château Grand-Puy-Lacoste	Pauillac
Château Grand-Puy-Ducasse	Pauillac
Château Haut-Batailley	Pauillac
Château Lynch-Bages	Pauillac
Château Lynch-Moussas	Pauillac
Château Dauzac-Lynch	Labarde-Margaux
Château Mouton-Baronne Pauline**	Pauillac
Château du Tertre	Arsac-Margaux
Château Haut-Bages-Liberal	Pauillac

continues

Table 5.2. Continued

Château	Commune
Château Pedesclaux	Pauillac
Château Belgrave	Saint-Laurent
Château Camensac	Saint-Laurent
Château Cos Labory	Saint-Estèphe
Château Clerc-Milon-Rothschild	Pauillac
Château Croizet-Bages	Pauillac
Château Cantemerle	Macau

**formerly known as Mouton-Baron Philippe

The 61 ranked wines are also known as Grands Crus Classés. While some vineyards have deteriorated or been incorporated into others, the rankings have been firmly set in stone with only one second growth, Château Mouton-Rothschild, ever changing its status; this wine was elevated to First Growth. Today there are rumblings about this rigidity as several châteaux have been improved by multimillion-dollar renovations to winery and vineyard and are politicking to be elevated to a higher status. As you may expect, considerable controversy is involved regarding the 1855 classification as many lesser classified growths feel worthy of elevation to a higher rank. To fully understand the honor of being one of the 61 Grands Crus Classés, remember that even in 1855, there were thousands of wine producers in Bordeaux.

You've probably noticed that with the exception of Château Haut-Brion, all of the wines listed are from the Médoc. Château Haut-Brion was included as it was considered one of the finest wines of Bordeaux as well as one of the most expensive; it could not be ignored. Only two regions were classified in 1855: the Médoc and Sauternes (a sweet wine area in southern Graves). Over the years, other regions, such as St. Émilion and Pomerol have been classified; however, with the exception of Château Pétrus and a handful of others, none of these wines compare with the First Growths of the 1855 Médoc classification.

Saint-Émilion and Pomerol

The districts of Saint-Émilion and Pomerol lie to the east of the city of Bordeaux. Picturesque Saint-Émilion is dotted with cafés that overlook the vineyards; here, you can sip your wine and watch it grow at the same time. Thousands of small châteaux cover the district, although only a handful can claim the best soil and microclimate for producing great wines. St. Émilion produces many fine wines (at least 40 excellent estates in this district), and it is classified with First growths; with rare exception, however, its First growths do not compare with the First growths of the 1855 Médoc classification.

Over the past two decades, the smaller and lesser known Pomerol has gained recognition from wine connoisseurs as its best wine, Château Pétrus, commands the highest price in Bordeaux. Several estates in Pomerol rival those of the 1855 Médoc classification, and many others produce some very fine wine. The soil here contains large amounts of clay in which Merlot grapes merrily grow. These grapes give the wines of Pomerol a character distinct from those of their Cabernet Sauvignon-producing neighbors.

Graves

The district of Graves, located along the southern edge of the city of Bordeaux, gets its name from its gravelly soil. Interestingly, the wines of Graves also seem to have a gravelly sense on the palate. Although Graves produces both reds and whites, it's most famous for its fine white wines. The main white grape varieties of Graves are

Sauvignon Blanc and Semillon. This blend works well because the Sauvignon Blanc offers immediate flavor and charm, while the Semillon adds body and depth to the wine.

Northern Graves, specifically the district of Pessac-Léognan, is home to producers of some of the world's most prestigious dry white wines. When young, the best dry white Graves are refreshing, crisp, and delightful. With age they mellow, developing complexity and richness. That said, a vast sea of mediocre, overly sulfured white wine still comes from this district, and you should be careful to choose Graves that come from modern producers.

Wine Wisdom

Dry white Bordeaux are well matched with shellfish, delicately flavored fish such as sole, and fresh fruit and berries. The lush, sweet Sauternes go with *pâté de foie gras*, rich *consommés*, full-flavored fish, mild cheeses, and, of course, sweet desserts. They're also wonderful all by themselves!

Sauternes—Where Noble Rot Reigns Supreme

Within the larger Graves district south of Bordeaux are the Sauternes and Barsac districts (districts within districts), which produce mostly sweet wines. This is where *noble rot* is at its most noble and prolific. The best Sauternes wines have a unique and luscious flavor thanks to the work of *Botrytis* (a plant disease caused by mold)—and the labor of vineyard workers who harvest the grapes.

Each berry is picked by hand, and only the fully mature berries are selected. The vineyard is harvested over and over, frequently 10 times or more at the best châteaux to select each grape as it matures.

This process is one reason why the best Sauternes—such as the region's most famous, Château d'Yquem—are so expensive. It pays to know your vineyards; some properties are more meticulous and obsessive with these procedures than others. The most outstanding (and expensive) Sauternes are produced by only a few vineyards in the district.

Where Are the Values?

If you're looking for a good buy in a Bordeaux wine, the rule is to avoid the classified crus. They are much in demand, and run from expensive to extremely expensive. A wine doesn't have to be in the 1855 classification to be enjoyable; in fact, those that aren't are not only drinkable long before their classified cousins, but are frequently almost as good.

Roughly 400 red wines make up the classification Cru Bourgeois, a classification of Bordeaux just below the 1855 classification. They generally sell for less than $20 (sometimes less than $10), and several can be comparable to or better than the lower-end classified growths. In addition, many red and white Bordeaux are referred to as *petits châteaux* that have no formal classification. Selling for $10 or less, these light-bodied wines are made to be enjoyed young. They're fine for an informal dinner at home.

Wine Wisdom

Red Bordeaux wines are a hearty and robust lot which go well with foods that stand up to them. If red meat is your meal of choice, you've met your match. Red Bordeaux are excellent with steak, rib roasts, venison, and lamb. They also go well with game birds; full-flavored, firm fish such as salmon; and cheeses such as brie, goat cheese, Swiss, and Parmesan.

When To Drink or Not To Drink

You might have to wait a lifetime to drink a Premier Cru unless you pay a fortune for a mature bottle, but many fine Bordeaux mature much sooner. Many of the lesser 1855 Cru Classé wines will be drinkable in five or 10 years, while others can take longer. Most petit châteaux, commune wines, and *négociant* blends are made for early consumption.

You can generally tell by the price of your wine and its classification (or lack of classification) whether it's ready for early consumption or yearns for solitude in a cellar. If a wine needs cellaring, drinking it before its time is more than infanticide—it's a waste of good wine. Such a wine will taste unpleasantly tannic and won't display its extraordinary qualities when too young.

Burgundy—
The Queen of Wine

Many Burgundy wines available in the United States are good, but not necessarily exceptional. In fact, some expensive Burgundies—at least, the ones produced by low-quality négociants and careless estates—can be downright awful. The best wines from Burgundy, however, are truly *vins extraordinaires*, standing among the most fascinating and complex of all wines.

Unfortunately for the consumer, the wines bear price tags to match their stratospheric status, and most importers and wine merchants refuse to handle such expensive wares in tiny amounts. So, unless you happen to be touring Burgundy or you've hit that winning lottery number, the *crème de la crème* of Burgundies may be beyond your grasp. That said, you can still enjoy some very pleasant red and white Burgundy wines without putting a severe dent in your wallet.

In this chapter, we'll cover Burgundy's five unique wine districts, each home to a number of small estates. You'll find out how the *terroir* (soil) affects the grapes grown on each estate, producing distinctively different wines, and learn the characteristics of fine red and white Burgundies. I'll also touch on the ultimate Burgundy bargain: Beaujolais, the inexpensive, refreshing, light-bodied red wine that's served chilled like a white. Part of the reason that it's a bit more difficult to find a fine, affordable Burgundy in the States is that these wines just aren't imported as much; compared with Bordeaux, the Burgundy region produces a lot less quality wine as well as considerably smaller quantities of wine. Beaujolais excluded (the Beaujolais district is technically part of Burgundy, but it produces a different type of wine), Burgundy produces only 25 percent as much wine as Bordeaux, and only a small portion of that makes up your better wines.

Burgundy Is Organized like This...

Vineyards in Burgundy are much smaller than those in Bordeaux. An estate of 50 or 60 acres represents a very large holding, and a vineyard owned by only one proprietor is the exception. Clos de Vougeot, for example, consists of 165 acres, and is owned by more than 80 different individuals. This can make it somewhat difficult to judge the quality of a wine by reading its label. (More on that later.)

As a reflection of the size difference between vineyard holdings in Bordeaux and in Burgundy, an estate in Burgundy is usually called a *domaine*, while the estates in Bordeaux carry the more majestic name *château*.

Burgundy is composed of five districts, all of which make distinctive wines:

➤ Mâconnais

➤ Beaujolais

➤ Chablis

➤ Côte Chalonnaise

➤ Côte d'Or

The Côte d'Or (literally "golden slope") is again divided into two parts:

➤ Côte de Nuits

➤ Côte de Beaune

Wine Wisdom

The term *Burgundy* usually refers to the red wines of the Côte d'Or and Côte Chalonnaise. The same is true for white Burgundy, which usually refers to the white wines of the Côte d'Or and Côte Chalonnaise. Chablis and Beaujolais are generally referred to by name. This rule isn't hard and fast, however, and after you become more familiar with wine jargon, you'll be able to pinpoint your Burgundy exactly.

The prime varietals of this region are Pinot Noir for red Burgundy and Chardonnay for white Burgundy. This is where that fussy vinifera, Pinot Noir, is on its best behavior and shows its most regal and charming character. The southern part of the Beaujolais district is home to the red Gamay grape.

The terroirs of Burgundy are tricky. Soils vary so much from one site to the next that, within one vineyard, two plots of the same varietal growing only a short distance from each other can yield two distinctively different wines. This is where it becomes important to understand fully how to read a Burgundy label. Two owners of the same vineyard do not necessarily produce the same quality or style of wines.

The AOC structure for Burgundy takes this inconsistency into consideration. In addition to the AOC tiers of Bordeaux, Burgundy tiers include AOC appellations for individual vineyard sites that are of exceptional quality. In Burgundy, the terms *Premier Cru* (First Growth) and *Grand Cru* (Great Growth—the highest quality) are official designations under AOC law. In Bordeaux, the same terms designate status imparted outside of AOC legislation.

Table 6.1 provides examples of AOC names in Burgundy from the most general to the most specific (for example, individual vineyard sites). The two broadest categories—regions and districts—represent approximately two thirds of all Burgundy wines. These wines range from $7 to $15 per bottle. Commune or village wines, such as Gevrey-Chambertin, comprise one-quarter of Burgundies, and retail for $15 to $30 per bottle. There are 53 communes in the Burgundy region with their own appellation.

Premier crus, such as Chassagne-Montrachet Les Pucelles, make up approximately 11 percent of Burgundy wines; the Premier Cru appellation has been given to 561 vineyards. These wines sell for $25 to $80 per bottle. The 32 Grand crus, such as Corton-Charlemagne or Le Montrachet, represent a mere 1 percent of Burgundy wines. Grand Cru prices begin at approximately $40 to $50 per bottle and can soar to $500 and more per bottle for Romanée-Conti (the most expensive Burgundy wine) and upwards of $3,000 per bottle for a mature wine of a great vintage.

Table 6.1. The Structure of Burgundy AOC Names

Specificity of Site	Examples
Region	Bourgogne Rouge
District	Côte-de-Nuits Villages; Mâcon-Villages
Village or Commune	Nuits St. Georges; Gevrey Chambertin; Fixin Premier Cru; Puligny Montrachet Les Pucelles; Beaune Clos-des-Ursules; Nuits St. Georges–Les Perrières
Grand Cru	Le Chambertin; La Romanée; Le Montrachet*

* These last two classifications refer to specific vineyards.

Generally, if the label of a Burgundy wine displays a vineyard *and* a commune name, it is either a Premier or Grand Cru. On most Premier Cru labels, the vineyard name is in smaller lettering than the commune name (although sometimes it may be the same size or larger). Grand Cru labels are more confusing; Grand Cru Burgundies with their own appellation may display only the vineyard name on the label with the term *Appellation Contrôlée* below the name, or they might also state *Grand Cru*. Wines with brand names might use only their name with an appellation. The way to tell the difference between brand-name wines and Grand Cru Burgundies is to look for quotation marks around a brand name and the name of a specific appellation in between the words *Appellation* and *Contrôlée*—for example, Appellation Meursault Contrôlée. When in doubt, check a good wine encyclopedia or a book on Burgundy.

Wine Wisdom

Some wines are made by blending the grapes of two or more Premier Cru vineyards in the same commune. These wines are still called Premier Crus, but instead of displaying the vineyard name, the label will have a commune name with the words *Premier Cru* or *1er Cru*. These wines generally come from négociants, but some come from growers who have tiny, lesser-known vineyards and would rather sell their wine simply as a Premier Cru.

A Fine White Burgundy Is like This

White Burgundy combines a silky mouthfeel with a fullness of flavor and lively acidity. The better appellations have a touch of oak. They develop complexity and finesse with age. Grands crus may require up to 10 years in the bottle, but most white Burgundy is ready to drink after two or three years. The aftertaste is frequently a lingering kaleidoscope of flavors—those of the primary taste as well as some new sensations. Chardonnay wines from elsewhere can achieve greatness, but there's nothing that can compare to great white Burgundy—except a great red Burgundy.

A Fine Red Burgundy Is like This

A fine red Burgundy is as different from its Bordeaux counterpart as night is from day. Because a red Burgundy is made from the Pinot Noir grape, it is lighter in color than red Bordeaux. It is medium-bodied to full-bodied, and is relatively low in tannin and often silky or velvety on the palate. The aroma is unique to Burgundy, with flavors that often resemble cherries and ripe berries or moss and woodsy mushroom scents. With age, a great Burgundy develops great complexity with subtle but memorable nuances of flavor and finesse. A red Burgundy requires from seven to 10 years to mature, and great Burgundies can continue to improve for decades.

The Wines of Burgundy

This section covers the principle wine districts of Burgundy. The wines from these districts are the ones that you will be most likely to find in the United States.

Grape Alert

You've probably seen California wines labeled *chablis* and *burgundy* (no capital letters). These domestic wannabes are simple, mass-produced jug wines that bear no resemblance to their Gallic namesakes: the 100 percent Pinot Noir Burgundy from Burgundy, France and the 100 percent Chardonnay Chablis from Chablis, France.

Mâcon-Villages

The Mâconnais district lies directly south of the Chalonnaise and north of Beaujolais. The winemaking center is the city of Mâcon, and the surrounding hills are replete with the chalky limestone beloved of Chardonnay grapes.

Mâcon-Villages wines are white wines (made from 100 percent Chardonnay grapes) with excellent value. Selling for $5 to $10 per bottle, they lack the complexity and distinction of the more expensive Pouilly-Fuissé wines, but they are lively and crisp and meant to be enjoyed young. Most are soft, round, and fruity. Unlike most Chardonnay wines (which are oaked), Mâcon-Villages wines offer an unoaked freshness.

The label will read Mâcon or Mâcon-Villages. Mâcon-Villages is a cut above mere Mâcon, and the best wines are those that come from a specific village; village names are added to the appellation: Mâcon-Viré, Mâcon-Lugny.

Pouilly-Fuissé

In the 1960s, Pouilly-Fuissé was an overpriced darling of wine importers; thankfully, it has returned to being a pleasant, unpretentious, and reasonably priced white wine.

Pouilly-Fuissé and Saint-Véran, two inner appellations within the Mâcon district, are made from Chardonnay grapes grown in a soil that imbues them with a unique quality. Both wines are similar to Chablis, but softer and less steely. Pouilly-Fuissé wines are mid-premium quality, usually selling for $15 to $25 per bottle. They are distinctly Chardonnay and have a crisp apple aroma, with a smooth texture and slight depth of flavor. Unlike the simple Mâcon wines, they are often oaked and are richer and fuller in body. The best quality wines come from the villages of **Solutré-Pouilly**, **Davayé**, and **Fuissé**. They possess more fruitiness and depth than Chablis, and the finish reveals a clean, earthy flavor. Within three or four years of aging, Pouilly-Fuissés develop a subtle degree of finesse. Saint-Véran wines are also an excellent value at $7 to $14 per bottle.

Beaujolais

You've probably seen the signs in the wine shops and restaurants every year around Thanksgiving proclaiming, "Beaujolais Nouveau is here!" Actually, the wine has nothing to do with our American holiday, other than fortuitous good timing.

Beaujolais wine, Nouveau or not, is made from the red Gamay vinifera, not Pinot Noir. Beaujolais and Beaujolais Supérieur (which has 1 percent more alcohol than simple Beaujolais) are district-wide AOC appellations; the wines come from the southern area of Beaujolais. The primarily clay soil in this district produces simple, light-bodied, fruity wines that sell for less than $8 per bottle and are best served no more than a year or two after their vintage. Unlike most red wines, they go well with light foods and are great to drink in warm weather.

Beaujolais Nouveau is only six weeks old when it begins to appear on Thanksgiving tables. Its vinous and fruity quality (very low in tannins) makes it a refreshing beverage on its own or with your favorite snacks. Don't even think of storing it; it is meant to be enjoyed within six months of the vintage.

Wine Wisdom

A young Beaujolais makes a good introductory red wine. If the very thought of Cabernet Sauvignon makes you pucker, try a Beaujolais first. Not all Beaujolais wines are light hearted. Wines carrying the appellation *Beaujolais-Villages* fall within the mid-premium range. Like their simpler cousins, they are fruity wines, but possess more depth, body, and structure than these related wines. Light in tannins, they can improve in bottle for two years or so.

Several communes in northern Beaujolais produce wines with potential mid-premium quality. These are the Crus

Beaujolais, which are distinctly better than Beaujolais-Villages. Only the name of the cru appears on the label, so you have to know the names of crus to know that they are Beaujolais wines.

Table 6.2, below, reviews the cru of Beaujolais. The crus are Brouilly, Chénas, Chiroubles, Côte-de-Brouilly, Fleurie, Juliénas, Morgon, Moulin-a-Vent, Regnié, and Saint-Amour. Wines from Brouilly and Fleurie tend to be elegant in style and very fragrant. Those from Moulin-a-Vent and Morgon offer rich flavor and style and are capable of longer aging. Over time, the best may resemble a village red Burgundy.

Table 6.2 The Cru of Beaujolais

Cru	Description
Brouilly	The lightest and fruitiest of the cru. Drink within two years.
Côte-de-Brouilly	A step better than Brouilly, fuller with more concentration; drink within three years.
Regnié	This is the newest addition to the Beaujolais cru. It is very similar to Brouilly in style and flavor.
Morgon	This cru resembles a red Burgundy more than a Beaujolais. It is full, rich, and earthy. Can age from five to eight years.
Chiroubles	Very delicate, flavorful, and perfumed. They are often super-premium wines. Drink within four years.

Cru	Description
Fleurie	Rich and flavorful with a medium body and velvety mouthfeel. Drink within four years.
Moulin-a-Vent	This is the richest and most concentrated of the cru. Powerful, with the capacity to age up to 10 years or more.
Chenas	Rich and flavorful. Similar to a Moulin-a-Vent. Drink within four years.
Julienas	Rich, full bodied and full flavored. One of the best of the cru. Drink within four years.
Saint-Amour	Light to medium body, soft and delicate. Drink within two years.

Beaujolais are sold primarily by large négociants—companies that buy grapes and wines from growers to blend, bottle, and sell under their own labels. Two of the premier négociants are Georges Duboeuf and Louis Jadot. These names on the label are reliable indicators of quality as the négociants do more than buy finished wine; they also work with the growers and set high standards for what they will buy. Higher-quality estate-bottled Beaujolais are also available, primarily imported by Kemit Lynch, Alain Junguenet, and Louis/Dresner Selections.

Wine Wisdom

Young and simple Beaujolais are closer to light white wines or rosés than to their more tannic red counterparts. They are best served chilled at about 55°F (13°C) to bring out their youthful vinous vitality. The fuller and more complex Cru Beaujolais should be served at the same temperatures as any red Burgundy: 60°F to 62°F (17°C).

Chablis

The village of Chablis, unfortunately and unjustly, shares its name with the best-known generic wine from the United States. This is where wine knowledge comes in very handy. The vineyards of Chablis are the northern-most in Burgundy, situated on the hills of the Serein River valley. There, the limestone soil and cooler climate impart a distinctive character to the Chardonnay grape. Chablis wines are also fermented differently than other Burgundy whites. While the white wines of the Côte d'Or are gener-ally fermented and aged in oak barrels, most Chablis winemakers have switched to stainless steel.

Chablis wines are light, austere, and crisp, with a charac-teristic bouquet and a steely taste resembling gunflint. Chablis is an excellent match for seafood, perfect if you're an oyster aficionado. Like other white Burgundies, Chablis is meant to be enjoyed cool but not cold (58°F to 60°F, or 15°C). The best Chablis wines come from a relatively small vineyard area. The finest Chablis, ranked as Grand Crus, develop a degree of elegance and style, though they are no match for their cousins of the Côte d'Or.

The Côte Chalonnaise

The Côte Chalonnaise is a Burgundy lover's dream—wines that are enjoyable and reasonably priced. They lack the refinement of the Côte d'Or wines, being somewhat coarser and earthier and with less perfume, but they make perfectly drinkable wines and you don't have to skimp on a meal to pay for them.

The district lies to the south of the Côte d'Or and has five appellations that produce quality wines for $8 to $20 per bottle.

➤ **Mercurey** Wines are mostly reds, some white. This is the home of the best Chalonnaise wines (at $15 to $20 per bottle).

➤ **Rully** About evenly divided between reds and whites. The earthy white wines are far superior to the reds.

➤ **Givry** Mostly red, some white. Here the reds are superior, although quite earthy.

➤ **Montagny** All white wines; pleasant and enjoyable.

➤ **Bouzeron** Wines from this district are frequently labeled as Bourgogne Rouge, Bourgogne Blanc, or Bourgogne Aligote (the other white grape that does well in Burgundy).

The Great Wines of the Côte d'Or

Wines from the Côte d'Or are unquestionably the most costly. Alas, this fact is often the result of overpricing rather than of outstanding quality. When they're right on target, Côte d'Or wines are superb. When they miss, they can range from very bad to dreadful, suffering from poor winemaking or an overly ambitious quest for big production. They should be subtle, replete with nuances, supple in texture, and unique in style.

Quality ultimately depends on the skill and integrity of the grower. The temperamental Pinot Noir grape does not leave any margin for error—one mistake and you're out. To avoid disappointment, familiarize yourself with small growers and producers. For a list of the best and most reliable producers and négociants, see Appendix B.

The Côte d'Or, where wine legends are made, is a narrow 40-mile strip consisting of two main subdivisions. The northern part is the Côte de Nuits, named for its commercial center, the city of Nuits-Saint-Georges. This is the home of some of the finest red Burgundies. The southern part is the Côte de Beaune, named for its most important city, Beaune. The Côte de Beaune is famous for both red and white wines, but its white Burgundies are especially celebrated.

The reds have a recognizably fruity, vinous aroma of Pinot Noir with the regional character of red Burgundies. The wines are straightforward, uncomplex, and reasonably well-balanced, with soft tannins and a lingering finish. Although sometimes coarse and lacking in finesse, they exhibit the character of the Burgundy region.

Mid-premium Burgundies from the Côte d'Or have two general appellations. Those from the larger place names will be called either Côte-de-Nuits or Côte-de-Nuits Villages, or Côte-de-Beaune or Côte-de-Beaune Villages. Wines with village names are usually slightly higher quality, although all fall within the same general range.

Côte de Nuits

The red wines from the Côtes de Nuits tend to be fuller-bodied, firmer, and more sharply defined than their southern counterparts from the Côte de Beaune.

Each wine district of the Côte de Nuits produces a unique wine.

Wines of the Côte de Nuits:

➤ **Gevrey-Chambertin** A rightfully famous wine village. Premier Cru wines are super-premium quality with great intensity of flavor and balance. Eight Grand Crus are labeled with the word *Chambertin*, alone or hyphenated as part of a vineyard name; outstanding examples include Chambertin and Chambertin-Clos de Beze. Complex, rich, harmonious, and beautifully structured, these particular Grand Crus combine power with finesse as they age.

➤ **Chambolle-Musigny** Delicate, feminine, soft, and elegant wines that possess great finesse. The Grand Cru vineyard, Le Musigny, produces a noble wine of uncommon breed, and is noted for its superb white as well as red Burgundies.

➤ **Vougeot** Home of the immense Grand Cru vineyard (by Burgundy standards) Clos de Vougeot. Quality varies, but Clos de Vougeot wines are enormously aromatic, sturdy, and complex. Most are medium-bodied and not as muscular as those of Chambertin; the finest have unquestionably noble bearing.

➤ **Flagey-Echézeaux** This commune contains two Grands Crus wines: Grand Echézeaux and Echézeaux—super-premium quality wines, aromatic, with a slightly more refined style than their Vougeot cousins.

➤ **Vosne-Romanée** Its Grands Crus—La Romanée-Conti, La Romaneée, La Tache, Richebourg, and Romanée-Saint-Vivant—are the stuff legends are made of. Rich, velvety wines combine depth and complexity of flavor from truffles, herbs, and berries. All of the Grands Crus—except the slightly lighter Saint-Vivant—usually achieve noble quality status. Tremendous aging potential.

➤ **Nuits-Saint-Georges** Contains no Grands Crus, but many Premiers Crus vineyards. Strongly aromatic, earthy, and often more tannic than wines of other communes, they possess a sturdy, full-bodied, very vinous flavor that comes into full harmony with long aging. If they're not noble wines, they're not far off the mark.

➤ **Fixin** The northernmost district in the Côte de Nuits. Produces sturdy, earthy red wines that do not develop finesse.

➤ **Morey-Saint-Denis** Produces full-bodied, sturdy, rich red wines. Grands Crus include part of Bonnes Mares, Clos des Lambrays, Clos de la Roche, Clos Saint-Denis, and Clos de Tart. These wines provide good value for the high quality they offer.

Côte de Beaune

The Côte de Beaune produces numerous Premiers Crus and super-premium red wines, but fewer Grands Crus wines. The red wines from the northern part of the Côte de Beaune, around Aloxe-Corton, are softer, fuller-bodied, and richer in flavor than the wines from the Côte de Nuits.

Similar to the Côte de Nuits, each wine district of the Côte de Beaune produces a unique wine.

The following lists wines of the Côte de Beaune:

➤ **Aloxe-Corton** Produces full-bodied, sturdy mid-premium wines labeled under the simple Corton appellation. The better Premiers Crus, Le Corton, Corton-Clos du Roi, and Corton-Bressandes are super-premium wines. Two superlative Grands Crus vineyards—Corton-Charlemagne and Charlemagne—offer Chardonnay wines of noble quality. These whites boast a rich, complex, perfumed aroma of fruit and butter, and their texture is oily, like butterscotch, with fine acid balance for structure and longevity.

➤ **Savigny-les-Beaunes**   A good value. Five of these wines are Premiers Crus, with superior delicacy and finesse. The wines labeled under the Savigny-les-Beaunes appellation are mid-premium quality.

➤ **Beaune, Côte-de-Beaune, or Côte-de-Beaunes Villages**   Beaune wines are medium-bodied, gentle reds and whites. Côte-de-Beaune Villages wines are generally mid-premium quality with some finesse and moderate aging potential. The Premiers Crus are complex wines, capable of combining great depth with a distinctive aroma, lightness of body with a firm structure.

➤ **Chorey-les-Beaune**   Red wines, similar to the Côtes-de-Beaune, that offer good value.

➤ **Pommard**   This village produces many mid-premium wines under its appellation. Wines can be village bottlings or from specific vineyards. These are full-bodied masculine reds. The Premiers Crus are fairly rich in aroma and body with a typical earthy finish. They age reasonably well and can aspire to super-premium status. Three recommended Grands Crus are Les Grands Epenots, Clos Blanc, and Les Rugiens.

➤ **Volnay**   Lightest in style of all Côte-de-Beaune wines, almost to the point of being fragile. Delicate and early maturing, Volnay Premiers Crus are soft and elegant reds with delicacy and finesse that places them in the super-premium division.

➤ **Auxey-Duresses**   Similar to wines of Volnay.

➤ **Auxey-Duresses, Monthelie, Saint-Romain, and Saint-Aubin** Little-known villages producing mostly red with some good white wines; they provide good value as they are not in much demand.

➤ **Pernand-Vergelesses** Another little-known district that provides good value in red and white wines.

➤ **Santenay** Lighter and more delicate, with less aging potential in the bottle.

➤ **Meursault** Offers some red wine, but is most famous for its white wines, which range from mid- to super-premium. Generally, wines labeled simply *A.C. Meursault* are mid-premiums—floral in character and streamlined in body with high, crisp acidity. The Premiers Crus of Meursault are the super-premiums, which display a silky texture, full body, assertive aroma, and complex flavors.

➤ **Puligny-Montrachet** White Burgundies that are created to perfection. Grands Crus—Le Montrachet, Bâtard-Montrachet, Chevalier-Montrachet, and Bienvenue-Bâtard-Montrachet—are legendary single-vineyard appellations capable of achieving noble quality. Le Montrachet and Bâtard-Montrachet cross over into Chassagne-Montrachet. These wines have a rich, complex, fruity aroma, often buttery in character, and combine depth of flavor with an intense but austere hard veneer. These unusually powerful white wines require upwards of 10 years of cellaring.

➤ **Chassagne-Montrachet** Offers some red wines, but is most famed for its stylish white wines, particularly the Premiers Crus (often super-premium wines), which are full and firm in structure with a distinct earthy flavor and character. Somewhat sturdier than Puligny, but with less finesse.

The Premiers Crus of both Puligny and Chassagne tend to be super-premium wines. Some, such as Les Combettes and Les Pucelles, have, on occasion, rivaled the Grands Crus in noble quality. Because the vineyards have so many different proprietors and these appellations are used by so many shippers, the names of owners and shippers become crucial quality determinants.

Where Are the Values?

In Burgundy, *value* is a relative term. The village and lesser-known appellations offer value-priced wines, but these don't display the qualities and subtleties for which Burgundian wines are so revered. When it comes to the Premiers and Grands Crus, the values are to be found in the vineyards and growers that are less in fashion; wines from the best growers, as well as most revered vineyard sites, command outrageously inflated prices. Finding the best values requires a familiarity with the numerous growers, their properties, and their reputations. Did I ever say learning about wine would be easy? Burgundy certainly presents the greatest challenge for the wine lover.

Chapter 7

Other Regions of France

· Sip ·

Bordeaux and Burgundy may be the chart toppers for French wines (still wines, that is; we'll get to the Champagne region later), but virtually all of France is replete with grape-growing terrain. In this chapter, we'll begin with the Loire Valley, the longest wine-producing region in the world. The grapes, flavors, and styles vary along with the scenery, providing us with a number of distinctive, enjoyable, and, best of all, affordable wines.

The Loire River Valley

Extending nearly 650 miles, the Loire River nurtures the world's longest viticultural region. The area is rich with vineyards, pleasant and agreeable wines, and magnificent castles and châteaux. The cool climate produces light-bodied refreshing white wines. If you want to savor your wine in its homeland, this is a fascinating region to visit. Below are the different districts of the Loire Valley.

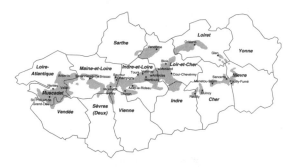

The Loire River nurtures the world's longest viticultural region.

Muscadet

Near the city of Nantes in the western part of the Loire Valley are vineyards producing the Muscadet or Melon grape. Muscadet wines are light-bodied, pleasant, slightly fruity wines. The best Muscadets are crisp and bone dry. Muscadet is an excellent companion to oysters, clams, and delicate fish. It's also a great summer drink.

Not only are Muscadet wines refreshing to drink, but their prices are equally refreshing. You can easily find a good Muscadet for $6 to $9. Buy it while it's still young—at its best, it retains a zesty effervescence and piquant vinosity for about one year from its vintage date. The best Muscadet wines will bear the name of the Sèvre-et-Maine region on the label. Also look for the term *sur lie*, which means that the wine was bottled right out of the cask. This procedure of "bottling off the lees" (the *lees* are the sediment of the wine) gives the wine freshness, and sometimes a lively slight prickle of carbon dioxide on the tongue. The most refreshing and flavorful Muscadet is bottled *sur lie* and is best drunk as early as possible.

Pouilly-Fumé

Pouilly-Fumé is a Sauvignon Blanc wine made in the vicinity of the town of Pouilly-sur-Loire. It is somewhat fuller and richer than Sancerre and can have spicy flavors with aromas of gunflint. Pouilly-Fumés range from slightly thin and ordinary wines to more aromatic and slightly complex premium wines; these wines can be quite fine when made by a good producer like Ladoucette. Pouilly-Fumé complements poached salmon, veal, or chicken.

The price range for Pouilly-Fumés is from $10 to $25 per bottle. It is best enjoyed young—within three or four years of the vintage.

Grape Alert

It's easy to mix up the names Pouilly-Fuissé and Pouilly-Fumé, but they are two very distinct wines. The Pouilly-Fuissé is made from Chardonnay grapes from the Mâcon in Burgundy and is a more full-bodied wine. The Pouilly-Fumé is made from Sauvignon Blanc grapes and is lighter and more refreshing.

Sancerre

In the eastern end of the valley, just south of Paris, are the towns of Sancerre and Pouilly-sur-Loire, located on opposite banks of the Loire River. Here, the Sauvignon Blanc grape thrives, making lively, dry wines that have spicy, green-grass flavors; these wines can range from ordinary to outstanding, and can be very distinctive. Compared to Pouilly-Fumé, Sancerre is somewhat lighter in body and more refreshing. It makes a good match for shellfish and delicate fish such as rainbow trout and is an enjoyable summer beverage. Sancerre wines fall into the same price range as Pouilly-Fumés. They are also best enjoyed within three or four years of their vintage.

Vouvray

The home of Vouvray wines is the central Loire Valley near Tours, is also home to palatial châteaux. Most Vouvray wines are white and made from the Chenin Blanc grape, which thrives on the formerly royal terrain. Generally, Vouvrays are reasonably priced at $6 to $10 per bottle. When young (a year or two from the vintage date), they are very pleasant. Although some Vouvrays are dry (usually marked *sec* on the label), typical Vouvrays will be slightly off-dry. They go well with white meats or fowl in rich butter or cream sauces. After dinner, try them with semifirm cheese, grapes, apples, pears, or any of your favorite fruits. Vouvray also produces inexpensive and pleasant sparkling wines.

Wine Wisdom

The wines of Vouvray are produced in three distinct styles—dry, medium-dry, or sweet (called *moelleux*)—which are luscious and are super-premium wines at their best. These sweet wines can only be made in vintages of unusual ripeness, which occur infrequently; thus, they are rare and costly.

The best-quality Vouvray wines are agers and require several years to develop. With their high acidity, they can last years without risk of becoming salad dressing. These bottle agers begin in the $12 to $17 per bottle price range.

Rosés of the Loire

The Loire Valley produces huge quantities of rosé wines. Most hail from an area around Anjou. The popular Anjou rosés are a lovely pink-orange color. They are low in acidity, appealingly fruity, and sometimes slightly spritzy. They range from slightly to very sweet in finish.

The Rhône River Valley

In southeastern France, south of Beaujolais and between the city of Lyon and the area of Provence, is the warm, sunny, and wine-rich Rhône Valley. The region consists of a northern and southern division, ironically separated by an area unsuitable for wine production. The regional reds are full, robust, and hearty with good color and a ripe, fruity character—not much complexity here, but there's nothing wrong with simple, straightforward red wine. The whites age well and are light- to medium-bodied, rich, and earthy.

The northern and southern Rhône Valley produce distinctively different wines. The greatest distinction, however, may be in the amount of wine each produces: The southern Rhône produces 95 percent of all Rhône Valley wine. The prime varietal in the southern Rhône is the Grenache, which produces wines with high alcohol content. Most Rhône wines are simple, inexpensive, and enjoyable—great for an informal evening at home. The following are descriptions of the different districts of the Rhône.

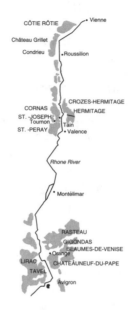

THE RHÔNE RIVER VALLEY

The Rhône Valley produces some superb wines.

Côtes-du-Rhône

The Côtes-du-Rhône and Côtes-du-Rhône Villages appellations encompass a wide range of highly drinkable red and white wines. Reds are more available in the United States, ranging from $5 to $12 per bottle. Wines from the higher appellation—the 17 villages that make up Côtes-du-Rhône Villages—are fuller and occupy the higher end of the price spectrum.

The reds are generally fruity and light-bodied, similar to inexpensive Beaujolais. Uncomplicated by nature, they can withstand a slight chilling to bring out their fruity vinosity, low acidity, and light tannins. The result is thoroughly pleasant drinking. The less-frequently found white

Côtes-du-Rhône bottlings are mildly fruity, and somewhat coarse and rough—but that's earthy wine at its best.

Gigondas and Vacqueyras

Gigondas and Vacqueyras are two former members of Côtes-du-Rhône Villages who now merit their own appellations. Gigondas, especially, is robust, rich, and a good ager. A quality vintage (1989 and 1990 are two prime choices) can thrive for 10 years or more in bottle. At $10 to $15 per bottle, it's an excellent buy.

Châteauneuf-du-Pape

Châteauneuf-du-Pape is the pride of the southern Rhône Valley. Its intriguing name evokes the 14th century, when the Popes resided on French soil in Avignon, and the vineyards with this regal appellation extended over 8,000 acres, producing more than a million cases of wine.

Châteauneuf-du-Pape is a robust red wine made from a blend of up to 13 grape varieties. The primary ones are Grenache, Mourvedre, and Syrah. Quality ranges from mid-premium to an occasional super-premium. At the upper levels are slow-maturing, hard, sturdy, tannic wines. The best are full-bodied, rich, complex, and high in alcohol. Some more accessible wines are fruitier, less complex, and rounder.

The best vintages age well in the bottle for 15 to 20 years. One of the finest Châteauneuf-du-Papes is Château Râyas, which differs from type by being 100 percent Grenache, made from very old vines. Château Beaucastel is a notable wine, which can mature for 20 years or longer.

Tavel and Lirac

A close neighbor of Châteauneuf-du-Pape, Tavel excels in producing the world's best—and most expensive—rosés. Less celebrated than Tavel, Lirac produces both reds and rosés. Lirac rosés are not equal in quality to their Tavel cousins, but they offer tasty, refreshing wines, and they are reasonably priced. The wines of both areas are made primarily from the Grenache and Cinsault grapes.

Hermitage

Hermitage reds are mid- to super-premium wines, rich and full-bodied with great aging potential. Made from the noble Syrah grape, they are not quite up to Côte-Rôtie wines in finesse, but are high in tannins and alcohol, and they develop complexity and vigor when fully aged. The best vintages will mature in the bottle for 30 years or more. (The years 1988, 1989, 1990, and 1991 were stellar years for the northern Rhône, and 1989 was the finest for Hermitage.) The three best producers of Hermitage are M. Chapoutier, Jean-Louis Chave, and Paul Jaboulet Aîné. The best Hermitages range from $35 to $60 per bottle, but Hermitages from lesser producers can be priced as low as $15 to $25 a bottle.

Hermitage also produces a small quantity of white wine, made from the Marsanne and Rousanne grape varieties. White Hermitage is a full, rich, earthy wine that needs six to 10 years to develop fully.

Condrieu

Condrieu, made 100 percent from the Viognier grape, is another excellent white wine from the northern Rhône. One of the most fragrant and floral wines you can find, it has delicate yet lush flavors, with fragrant, fresh apricot and peach nuances. Condrieu sells for about $18 to $25 per bottle; it's a wine to drink young.

Côte-Rôtie

Côte-Rôtie wines are almost uniformly high in quality—many reach super-premium quality. They are more subtle than Hermitage wines; firm and long lasting, they develop a berry and truffle flavor with aging, and their smooth texture gives them finesse as they mature.

Peak vintages (1991 was a prime year) of Côte-Rôtie possess aging potential of 20 years or more. The most celebrated producer of Côte-Rotie is Guigal. La Mouline, La Landonne, and La Turque, Guigal's single vineyard wines, are superb (though quite expensive). The range for most Côte-Rôties is between $20 and $45 per bottle.

Alsace—the German Wines of France

Located near Germany in the northeast corner of France, Alsace is set apart from the rest of France by the Vosges Mountains. Alsace became part of France in the 17th century, to be reclaimed by Germany in 1871, and then lost to France once again after World War II. Less than 50 years of German rule over a span of three centuries may seem like a short time, but the Germans had an impact, at least on the wine: The style and character of Alsatian wines is much closer to German wines than to their French counterparts. Like Germany, Alsace produces primarily white wines.

Wines from Alsace differ further from other French wines in that almost all Alsatian wines carry a grape variety name and bear an appellation, which is simply *Alsace*. Also, Alsatian wines come in a tall, thin tapered bottle called a *flute*, which is different from any other bottle in France.

Alsatian vineyards are largely populated by German grapes—Riesling, Sylvaner, Gewürztraminer—along with some Pinot Blanc, Pinot Gris, Pinot Noir, and Muscat varieties. The small quantity of light-bodied Pinot Noir is vastly outnumbered by the 93 percent of white Alsatian wines. The climate of Alsace and the vinification of its grapes endow the Alsatian whites with a fuller body, stronger alcohol content, and greater austerity and dryness than their German counterparts. The Alsatian whites, Gewürztraminer especially, have a spicy character unique to the region.

Riesling

Riesling, produced in a relatively dry style, is the king of wines in Alsace (as it is in Germany). Alsatian Riesling has a flowery bouquet as well as a firmness that belies its flavors. Most Alsatian Rieslings are meant to be consumed young; wines from outstanding vintages, however, are produced in a late-harvest style and can be aged for a decade or more. Rieslings cost approximately $10 to $20 per bottle, with late-harvest bottlings going for upwards of $50 per bottle.

Gewürztraminer

For dry, spicy Gewürztraminer, Alsace has no equal. The Gewürztraminer grape has a personality all its own: pungent and intense with a unique spicy flavor. You either like it or you don't. High in alcohol and low in acidity, its impression is rich and mellow. Gewürztraminer goes well with strong cheeses, spicy Asian cuisine, and your favorite fruit; it's also fine all by itself before or after a meal. It sells in the same price range as Riesling, but is not as much of an ager.

Pinot Blanc

Alsatian Pinot Blanc is the lightest of the region's wines and has a mellow fruity character. Although it is generally dry, some producers make their Pinot Blanc medium-dry to appeal to wine drinkers who don't like such an austere style. You can't tell from the label which style is which, so you should ask your wine merchant about the tastes of particular brands. In either style, these wines are best drunk young. Pinot Blanc ranges from $5 to $15 per bottle.

Other Varieties

The Sylvaner grapes make slightly fruity, highly acidic table wines. Only a small quantity is sold in the United States. Similarly, Muscat d'Alsace, a slightly bitter, usually dry white wine is found here only in small quantities. Tokay d'Alsace, made from Pinot Gris, is a full-bodied, rich, and spicy wine that has a lot to offer. Like Gewürztraminer, it is low in acidity and high in alcohol. It sells in the $8 to $15 category and makes a good complement for spicy meat dishes.

Les Autres

Les Autres translates simply as "the others." The two areas in this section—Côtes-de-Provence and Pays D'Oc, each of which is described next—produce simple, affordable wines.

Côtes-de-Provence—Land of Sunshine

Côtes-de-Provence is located in the south of France, bordering the French Riviera in the hilly region between Marseilles and Nice. It produces vast quantities of refreshing, simple red, white, and rosé wines, along with tiny amounts of sparkling wine.

The white wines are labeled either *Côtes-de-Provence* or *Cassis*. When well made, these relatively dry wines are fruity and pleasingly refreshing, with some amount of distinction. White wines from the Appellation Contrôlée Cassis tend to be more austere and richer in flavor. The numerous rosés from this region are uncomplicated and dry to slightly off-dry. The red wine from Bandol, made primarily from the Mourvedre Franc varietal, is tasty and pleasant, although it tends to be overpriced.

Vin de Pays D'Oc—Simple Wines for Every Day

This is one of many districts in the large Languese-Roussillon region of central France, formerly known only for very cheap *vin ordinaire*. Thanks to innovation and technology (and maybe some strong motivation on the part of the region's winemakers), the wines have been upgraded in quality. They are straightforward, simple wines, reasonably priced and fine for everyday drinking. They range in price from $4 to $10 per bottle and frequently offer fine value. Other wines similar in quality are Faugeres, St. Chinon, Fitou, Corbières, Minervois, Côtes-du-Roussillon, Coteaux du Languedoc, Pic-St.-Loup, and Vin de Pays de L'Heroult.

Chapter 8

O Solo Mio

In This Chapter

➤ Italian wine laws

➤ The major wine regions of Italy

➤ Deciphering the Italian wine label

With grape vines growing virtually everywhere, Italy boasts of producing more wine than any other country in the world. No Italian meal is complete without the clinking of wine glasses.

Yet, surprisingly, Italy is a relative newcomer to the world wine market. For generations, Italians kept the best premium wines for their own consumption. Although the Italian winemaking tradition goes back three millennia to the Etruscans, Italy's formal system of classification goes back only three decades. Today there is still no equivalent to the French *cru* system of vineyard classification. It is, however, possible to find great Italian wines with breed and finesse; it just requires some homework, and you'll learn the basics in this chapter.

Italy has 20 wine regions, which correspond to its political sectors. Wine regions here are called *zones*, to avoid political connotation.

The best of Italy's wine districts.

Getting a Basic Handle on Italian Wines

For our purposes, Italy's wines fall into three categories:

➤ Inexpensive red and white wines often sold in magnums (wine bottles that contain two regular-sized bottles of wine, about 1.5 liters total) for everyday drinking.

➤ Better wines, which range from simple to mid-premium quality.

➤ A small, select number of world-class wines that are of super-premium quality and, on occasion, noble quality.

In the first category is one of the best-known Italian wines for casual drinking: Lambrusco. This wine, which is an effervescent, slightly sweet red wine, rose to popularity in the United States in the 1970s and continues to please drinkers who want a pleasant, undemanding wine. In the second category are most of the Italian wines described in this chapter, and many other wines that space does not permit us to discuss. The third category includes wines that have been created to emulate the finest wines of Bordeaux and California as well as the best home-grown wines of Italy: Barolo, Barbesco, Gattinara, and Brunello. These new kids on the block have been receiving acclaim worldwide and have brought a new respect to the Italian wine-producing community.

Italian Wine Laws

For many years, all Italian wines were equated with a cheap and largely undrinkable product sold in straw-covered flasks under the blanket label *Chianti*. Although some of these wines were actually from Chianti, many were not. Not surprisingly, a great number of Italian winemakers who took pride in their wares considered themselves unfairly stigmatized. To correct the unfortunate impression, and to provide a viable structure for the Italian wine industry, the Italian government enacted a body of laws called the *Denominazione di Origine Controllata* (DOC). First introduced in 1963, DOC laws were implemented in 1967.

DOC laws control the quality of Italian wines by legally defining viticultural districts; by controlling the principal yield per acre, grape varieties, and alcohol content; and by setting minimum requirements for cask aging. The terms *Superiore*, *Riserva*, and *Classico*, which appear on wine labels, are now endowed with legal significance.

There are three categories of Italian wines:

➤ **Simple table wine**   For the most part, these non-DOC wines do not come to the United States.

➤ **DOC wine**   Most imported Italian wines are DOC, which is a large category spanning the quality range from simple everyday wines to super-premiums. There are currently more than 250 DOC-designated districts, and you'll see the phrase *Denominazione di Origine Controllata* on the labels of their wines. As with French regulations, specific requirements for each DOC vary. An appellation of a Classico region, which has more stringent standards than the broader DOC, provides a two-tiered rank order—for example, Chianti Classico.

➤ **DOCG wine**   Above the basic DOC classification is a designation given to only 13 wines: *Denominazione di Origine Controllata e Garantita* (DOCG). These elite wines, mostly in the super-premium quality category, must meet all the requirements of the DOC, then meet higher standards of winemaking practices, and finally pass a taste test. DOCG wines that fail to pass the taste test are declassified as ordinary table wine rather than DOC wine. Obviously, this motivates winemakers to produce a superior product. Tasting requirements do not, however, guarantee superior quality; too much depends on the qualifications of the taster, the tasting methods, and the taste standards employed—all the more reason to be informed about your wine.

Italy's Major Wine Regions

Italy has hundreds of wine districts, too many to cover in this book. I'll cover the most well-known districts that produce the most readily available (in the United States) wines

Tuscany—Art, Antiquity, and Chianti

Tuscany is one of Italy's foremost wine districts. It is home to Chianti, perhaps the most famous wine of Italy, as well as other wines which are described in the following sections.

Chianti

The best wines of Tuscany come from Chianti, the largest DOC zone; the Chianti vineyards are situated among olive groves, stone farmhouses, and an occasional castle, and are not far from Florence. It's only a short hop from Chianti's bucolic, picturesque vineyards to some of the world's most impressive art and architecture.

Chianti is divided into seven sub-districts: Classico, Colli Fiorentini, Montalbano, Rufina, Colli Aretini, Colli Senesi, and Colli Pisani. All of them turn out good wine (in fact, all hold DOCG status), but Chianti Classico is the undisputed Numero Uno. Second in quality is Chianti Rufina. Chianti wines may carry the name of the district, or may appear simply as *Chianti*.

Wine Wisdom

At any price, Chianti is a great value. A simple Chianti sells for about $6 per bottle. Chianti Classico is usually in the $8-to-$15 range, and well worth it. From there it's only a brief step to Chianti Classico Riservas, which are only $2 over the price of the regular Chianti Classico.

Chianti wines vary according to sub-district and, to a lesser degree, grape blending. They also vary in style and quality. Ordinary Chianti, at the lower end of the price range, is a prickly, fruity wine, meant to be drunk young. The middle range encompasses simple to mid-premium wines, Classico or otherwise, which age well in the bottle for several years, but can also be enjoyed when you buy them. The highest quality is the Riserva, the product of a special selection of vines or harvest, greater TLC in winemaking, and longer aging before release (at least three years). Riservas are frequently aged in French oak for a minimum of 10 years. Many will age well for 20 or 30 years.

Montalcino

Chianti is not the only red wine of Italy—it just seems like it is. One important Tuscan red wine, currently basking in glory, hails from the town of Montalcino, south of Florence in the Siena hills. This relative newcomer emerged from a clone or variant of the Sangiovese, known as the Brunello (or large Sangiovese). The resulting wine, Brunello di Montalcino, is a huge full-bodied and intense wine with concentration and astringent tannins that require aging of up to 20 years when made traditionally. There is general agreement that Brunello di Montalcino has the potential to be one of the world's most superb and long-lived red wines. Prices begin at $25 to $40 per bottle and scale upward. Rosso di Montalcino is a less expensive wine made from the same grapes, and the same production area, as Brunello di Montalcino. From a good producer, this wine will provide you with a hint of what Brunello tastes like at an affordable price ($10 to $15 per bottle).

Montepulciano

From vineyards surrounding the hill town of Montepulciano comes another red wine, Vino Nobile di

Montepulciano. Vino Nobile is close to a Chianti Classico and responds better to aging. Its minimum age is two years; a *Riserva* must have three years, and with four it can be designated *Riserva Speciale*. Just as there is a younger and lighter version of Brunello, there's a version of Vino Nobile as well: Rosso di Montepulciano.

Carmignano

This district, west of Florence, produces a red wine that owes a good part of its high quality to the incongruous but welcome presence of Cabernet Sauvignon. Essentially a Chianti with a French flair, Carmignano can be made with up to 10 percent of the noble Bordeaux grape.

San Gimignano

Possibly a descendant of the white wine of the Etruscans, Vernaccia di San Gimignano bears the name of a medieval walled village west of the Chianti Classico zone. Vernaccia is vinified to be drunk young. It is a refreshing white wine with a slightly viscous texture and hints of almonds and nuts. Most Vernaccias cost about $6 to $8 per bottle.

Super-Tuscans

During the 1970s, certain visionary winemakers decided to transcend the limits of traditional winemaking and experiment with unorthodox blendings in a quest to make wine of Bordeaux classified–growth stature. Producers such as Piero Antinori gained worldwide attention by creating new wines (for example, Tignanello and Solaia) that became known collectively as super-Tuscans. Like Carmignano, these blends were usually Sangiovese and Cabernet Sauvignon.

Today, there's considerable variance in the blends of the super-Tuscans. Some producers use Cabernet Sauvignon; others use Merlot or Syrah, while still others stick to native Tuscan varieties. There's considerable variance in price, too: from $30 or $40 up to $75 or $100 per bottle. No doubt about it, these wines are not cheap. The common denominator is that they are all of superb quality—super-premium and sometimes better. The most famous super-Tuscan wines, Sassicaia and Solaia, are much sought after by wine aficionados and can cost upwards of $200 in great vintages.

Piedmont—Home of Barolo, Barbaresco, and Gattinara

Situated in northwest Italy and bordering France and Switzerland in an area that combines agriculture, industry, and mountaineering, Piedmont is the site of two very important wine zones: Alba, which is known for its red wines, and Asti, famous for its sparkling wines.

Some wine lovers call Piedmont the noble wine region of Italy, a reputation it owes to the noble Nebbiolo varietal. This sensitive grape is the pride of Piedmont—nowhere else does it really strut its stuff.

Wine Wisdom

The red Nebbiolo grape is the heart of three of Italy's best DOCG wines: Barolo, Barbaresco, and Gattinara. Fine Barolo and Barbaresco are pricey at $25 to $45 per bottle, but worth it if they're from a good producer and vintage. Gattinara offers Nebbiolo style and verve at a more palatable price: $12 to $18 per bottle.

Barolo and Barbaresco

Both Barolo and Barbaresco wines come from the central part of the Piedmont region. Made entirely from Nebbiolo grapes, they hail from the Langhe hills near Alba. Both wines are full-bodied and robust—high in tannins, acidity, and alcohol. Their aromas evoke hints of tar, violets, strawberries, and black truffles. Barbaresco tends to be less austere than Barolo and slightly lower in alcoholic content. It is softer and more delicate, and can be consumed earlier.

Traditionally made Barolo and Barbaresco are agers; some (Barolo especially) need 10 or more years of aging before they are ready to drink. They should be opened a few hours before drinking to receive adequate aeration. Some producers are making these wines in a Bordeaux style so that they are enjoyable sooner, and are using French oak barrels for aging to give the wine an oaked character.

Barbera

Roughly half of Piedmont's wine production comes from the Barbera grape. A rich, fruity wine with high acidity but little tannin, Barbera is the everyday table wine of Piedmont. Barbera d'Alba is somewhat richer than the more austere Barbera d'Asti. Barbera has recently soared in popularity in the United States, which means that it's widely available and reasonably priced. You can get two types of Barbera: The traditional style is aged in large oak casks, which impart only a minimum of oak flavor; these wines retail for $8 to $15 per bottle. The newer style is aged in *barriques* (French oak barrels). The smaller containers endow the wine with oakier flavor and a higher price tag: $20 to $40 per bottle. Although oaky is "in" in some circles, both you and your wallet might prefer tradition.

Dolcetto

If you know some Italian and you think "Dolcetto" refers to a sweet wine, you'll be surprised. Actually, it's the grape that's sweet; the wine is uniquely dry. It's vinous in quality, low in acidity, and rich in soft tannins. Dolcetto is another favorite everyday wine, and it's easy to drink—even with its slightly bitter undertone. Some wine enthusiasts like to compare Dolcetto to Beaujolais, but Dolcetto is usually drier and makes a better complement to a meal. Dolcetto sells for about $10 to $12 per bottle; the best Dolcetto wines are Dolcetto d'Alba, which most good Barolo makers produce.

Nebbiolo d'Alba

Lighter in body than Barolo or Barbaresco, this Piedmont red often has a sort of fruity, sweet undertone. It retails in the $10 to $15 range, and it's worth a try.

The Queen of Hearts from Alice's Wonderland would have been happy in Piedmont; no doubt about it, reds dominate. There are, however, two white wines worth trying:

- ➤ **Gavi** This very dry, refreshing wine with high acidity is named for a town in southern Piedmont. Most Gavis sell for $10 to $15 per bottle, but some of the best examples go for as much as $35 per bottle and are worth the price.

- ➤ **Arneis** The white wine is from the Roero zone near Alba. Named for the grape from which it's made, Arneis is a medium-dry to dry wine with a rich flavor and texture. It reveals its best qualities when consumed within a year of the vintage. It sells for $12 to $18 per bottle.

Friuli–Venezia Giulia

Nestled up against Austria and Slovenia, this prolific winemaking zone has been letting the world know that Italy's wines come in two colors: white and red. Roughly four times as many white wines are produced here as reds. Over the last 20 years, white wines from Friuli–Venezia Giulia (better known in our country as simply Friuli), have been making their way to New World shores and stores.

The districts of Collio and Colli Orientali del Friuli are the top winemaking districts in Friuli. Their cool climate produces wines that are crisp and clean. The grapes of Friuli include Riesling (both Rhein and Italico), Müller-Thurgau, Chardonnay, Sauvignon Blanc, Pinot Bianco, and Pinot Grigio. Add to this impressive area of white varietals two local winners: Tocai Friulano and Ribolla Gialla.

And now for something really different: One Friuli wine that falls into no category is Picolit, an unusual (and expensive) white dessert wine. It makes a good conversation piece when wine lovers gather.

Umbria—Home of Orvieto

To the south of Tuscany, almost in the center of Italy, lies Umbria. According to legend, its best-known wine, the white Orvieto, has been produced since Etruscan times. It's made from the Trebbiano grape, and the vineyards are planted in volcanic rock, which gives the wine a distinctive, earthy character. Orvieto also has a Classico zone and is produced as both a dry and a semi-dry wine. You can find a good Orvieto for less than $10.

Sicily and Sardinia

Although Sardinian wines have achieved some popularity in the United States, most of them are merely ordinary. Sicily, however, does produce some interesting wines, notably from Regaleali's vineyards, which are situated intriguingly on the slopes of Mount Etna. The white DOC wines of Etna have a volcanic character, which makes them particularly attractive and worth a try.

Regaleali produces red, white, and rosé wines; these range from mediocre to extraordinary, and some of the reds are among Italy's finest wines. Try Rosso del Conte, the best red wine from one of Sicily's noted producers: Count Regaleali. He also makes a Chardonnay that rivals those

of the Côte D'or, and a dry *rosato* (rosé) that sells for
about $8.

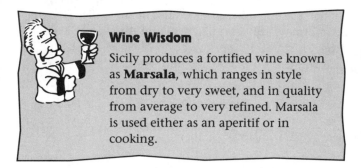

Wine Wisdom

Sicily produces a fortified wine known
as **Marsala**, which ranges in style
from dry to very sweet, and in quality
from average to very refined. Marsala
is used either as an aperitif or in
cooking.

Some good sparkling wines hail from Sicily, ranging from
the *brut* (dry) to the sweet, such as the muscat-flavored
spumantes from the Island of Pantellaria.

We Next Play Veneto

The best wines from the Veneto zone come from vineyards surrounding the beautiful city of Verona. Verona's
three leading wines are among the most well known and
widely available in our country: the reds, Valpolicella and
Bardolino, and the white, Soave. Too bad the Montagues
and the Capulets didn't raise a glass to settle their differences.

➤ **Bardolino**   Made primarily from the Corvina
   grape variety, Bardolino is named for the charming
   village situated on Lake Garde. It also has a Classico
   zone where the better wines are made. Bardolino is a
   light, fruity wine that is pleasant when young; it's
   closer in style to Beaujolais than to its Corvina
   cousin, Valpolicella. Try a chilled Bardolino on a hot
   summer evening—and imagine you're on the beautiful lake in the Italian countryside.

➤ **Valpolicella** The Valpolicella district resides on a series of hills, some of which overlook Verona. Valpolicella is also made mainly from the Corvina grape, but is fuller in body than Bardolino, with more color, alcohol, durability, depth, and complexity. Those labeled *Classico* come from the best growing area; the exception is Valpantena, made from grapes grown in a valley to the east. It doesn't have the Classico label, but its quality is as good as Classico—and sometimes better. If you see *Superiore* on the label, let the bottle age for a minimum of a year. Some Valpolicellas improve in the bottle for several years.

➤ **Recioto** Another classification of Valpolicella, Recioto is made from grapes that are grown high up on the hillside, and then dried on straw mats in lofts or attics to concentrate their sugars and fruits before vinification. Recioto contains about 14 to 16 percent alcohol, and is made in three different styles:

> **Sparkling wine** This is rarely seen in the United States.

> **Recioto** Called simply Recioto, this style is sweet because fermentation stopped or "stuck" before all the sugar was fermented.

> **Amarone Recioto** Also called *Amarone della Valpolicella* or just *Amarone*, this is one of the special wines of Italy that deserves super-premium classification. Amarone is completely fermented and is velvety, round, soft, well-balanced, and full of character. You can age a good Amarone 10 to 15 years, but most are delightful after only five.

➤ **Soave** This easy-to-drink neutral white wine comes from an area near Valpolicella. Made predominantly from the Garganega grape, along with some Trebbiano, Soave is available as both Classico and non-Classico wine. Most of the better Soaves come from the Classico zone, an area to the northeast of the picturesque town of Soave itself.

No doubt Americans not only love the pleasant flavor of Valpolicella, Bardolino, and Soave, but the price as well: Most retail in the $5 to $8 range. Two other white wines of the region, Bianco di Custoza and Lugana, fall into the same range.

The Northern Climes— Trentino–Alto Adige

Trentino–Alto Adige, located at the top of the "boot," is actually two very distinct zones: the Italian-speaking Trentino to the south, and the primarily German-speaking Alto Adige (or South Tyrol) to the north. Not surprisingly, the wines of both zones are as distinctly different as the languages.

Most of the red wine made in this border region goes to Austria. Its white wines rival those of Friuli. Pinot Grigio, Chardonnay, and Pinot Bianco from Alto Adige retail in the $6 to $15 range and have pleasant melon-like overtones.

Lombardy

Once famous for its expert craftsmen, Lombardy is less well known for its wine, although some delightful red and white wines come from this region. The best white wine is Lugana, produced from the slopes bordering Lake Garda. Four mid-premium reds come from the Valltellina region, high up in the pre-Alps, just below the Swiss border. The predominant grape is Nebbiolo, known here as Chiavennasca. The four light-bodied red wines are Sassella, Inferno, Grumello, and Valgella. All are highly drinkable and affordable, too: usually under $10. These wines can be consumed a year or two from the vintage.

Latium

Latium (or Lazio) is the area around Rome. The best-known wine is Frascati, made from the Trebbiano grape and produced on the volcanic slopes of the Colli Romani southwest of Rome. Named for the town Frascati, the wine should be light, fresh, charming, and fragrant. It is usually dry (labeled *asciutto* or *secco*), although sweeter versions are made too (*cannellino*, *dolci*, or *amabile*). It's meant to be enjoyed young (a year or two from the vintage). Vast quantities of Frascati are produced and quality can be variable.

Emilia-Romagna

This region is famous for the city of Bologna and the ocean of soft, effervescent Lambrusco wine it produces each year.

Abruzzo

Abruzzo is best known in the United States for the red Montepulciano d'Abruzzo. This very inexpensive wine is frequently sold in magnums for $4 to $6. It is easy to drink with low tannins and low acidity.

Marche (The Marches)

Left out of most travel itineraries and devoid of any great historical attractions, its white wine, Verdicchio, put Marche on the map. The most famous comes from Verdicchio dei Castelli di Jesi, a large wine zone. It's made mainly from the Verdicchio grape, with up to 20 percent of the Trebbiano Toscano and the Malvasio Toscano grapes permitted. It's a dry, simple wine to be enjoyed young (within two years, at the latest).

Campania

This is the area around Naples, the land of Mount Vesuvius. From the northeast of the city come some outstanding wines, ranging from mid-premium to, at times, noble quality. These are the work of Antonio Mastroberardino; his name may be difficult to pronounce, but his wines are worth the vocal gymnastics.

Greco du Tufo and Fiano di Avellino are Mastroberardino's unique whites. Greco is viscous and quite strong in bouquet and flavor; sometimes it is also strong in alcohol, but it's always well balanced. Its flavors have a bitter almond edge, which increases with bottle age. It retails in the $12 to $18 range. Fiano has greater elegance of body and texture and a sort of toasty bouquet.

Despite the excellence of the two whites, Mastroberardino's ultimate work of art is the rich, full-bodied, and tannic Taurasi. This DOCG wine is made from the Aglianico grape grown at altitudes of 1,000 feet or higher. Great vintages of Taurasi age well for 10 or 20 years and can attain near noble status. The single-vineyard Taurasi wine, Radici, is especially recommended.

Apulia and Basilicata—The Southern Tip

Along with Calabria, the regions of Apulia and Basilicata in the south of Italy are mainly responsible for Italy's well-known comparison to a boot (they are the shoe part), and for producing a sea of wine.

Apulia is essentially a gigantic vineyard, but only in the past two decades have modern winemaking techniques resulted in wines of note. Formerly heavy in alcohol and often sunbaked, the trend in Apulia has been toward fruitier, fresher, lighter wines. The Aleatico di Puglia grape is used to make a red DOC dessert wine. Basilicata is distinguished by the production of Aglianico del Vulture, a superb DOC red wine that improves with age. This mid-premium wine is quite smooth and has a caramel background and lots of fruit.

¡Olé!—Wines in the Spanish Style

Table wines from Spain, Portugal, and Chile all share attributes; their tastes, flavors, and styles are relatively similar and they all offer excellent value for your money. Look to these wines for everyday drinking.

The wines in this chapter range from the traditional wines of Spain (the red Rioja) and Portugal (the Dao) to the eclectic wines of Chile, where viticulture introduced by Spanish settlers has been transformed by centuries of successive generations of immigrants. All of the countries covered in this chapter produce substantial quantities of agreeable, worthy wine—and all deserve greater visibility worldwide.

Spain...¡Olé!

Despite the fact that Spain ranks third (after Italy and France) in world wine production, few Americans are familiar with any Spanish wines beyond the fortified Sherry and the red Rioja. In today's market, Spain offers a wide variety of wine styles, and with good, careful selection, you'll find an impressive array of wines at excellent values.

One obstacle to the wine world's recognition of Spain has been the country's lack of a uniform regulatory system, coupled with a laxity of enforcement where laws existed. This laxness is in the process of changing considerably. Spain's wine laws, like Italy's, have a dual-level classification: *Denominaciones de Origen* (DO) and the higher classification *Denominaciones de Origen Calificada* (DOCa). The higher tier was added in 1991, and its only occupant to date is Rioja, the popular red wine from the Rioja region. Wines with no DO classification fall into the category of table wines, *Vino de la Tierra*, which is comparable to the French *Vins de Pays*.

Here are few terms to help you decipher a Spanish wine label:

➤ **Crianza** On a bottle of red, it means that the wine has been aged for at least two years, including a period of oak aging; on a bottle of white or rosé, it means that the wine is a minimum of one year old.

➤ **Reserva** Red Reservas are aged in oak and in bottle for a minimum of three years; white and rosé Reservas are aged for at least two years, including six months in oak. Reservas are produced only in good vintages.

➤ **Gran Reserva** Red wines are aged in oak and in bottle for a minimum of five years; white and rosé Gran Reservas are aged at least fours years, with a minimum of six months in oak. Gran Reservas are made only in exceptional vintages.

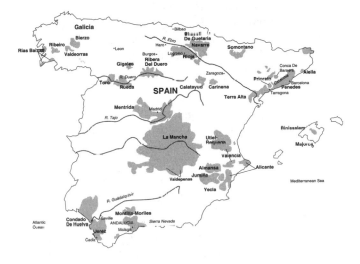

The regions of Spain's finest wines.

Rioja

Rioja has recently seen the transition from traditional to modern winemaking—with impressive results. Using the traditional method, making red Rioja meant years of aging in small oak barrels (interestingly, American oak); the resulting wine was too often mediocre and flat, suffering the combined effects of overaging and poor winemaking. The modern trend is to replace cask aging with stainless steel and bottle aging, resulting in fresher, crisper, fruitier wines. In the traditional style, there has been movement away from American oak to French oak, which imparts more character to the wine.

Before modernization and DOCa classification, the term *Reserva* on a red wine label was a statement of aging only, not quality. That rule has changed. Now the term Reserva, used exclusively for red wines, also denotes a minimum level of quality (as well as three years of aging).

There are several types of red Riojas. Some Riojas are young wines with no oak aging; others, labeled *Crianza*, are aged by the vintner in oak and in bottle for two years. The finest Riojas are aged five years or longer and bestowed with the status *Gran Reserva*.

Penedes

The Penedes region in Catalonia, south of Barcelona, isn't as famous as Rioja, but it's easily *the* region in Spain for table wines. Its two leading producers, Torres and Jean Leon, are both known for their outstanding red wines, which start in the $6 to $8 range; the better wines go for up to $30 a bottle. These wines are made in both varietal renditions as well as blends.

A sizable percentage of Spain's sparkling wine emanates (or effervesces) from the Penedes. The leading producers are in the town of San Sadurni do Noya, located in the El Penedes Central; Cordorniu, the world's largest producer of sparkling wines by the *methode champenoise* (champagne method), and Freixenet, which is growing in production and popularity, are both here.

Wine Word

To understand Spanish wines, know these terms: *Cosecha* or *Vendimia* denotes the vintage year; *Bodega* means winery; *Tinto* means red; *Blanco* is white; *Viejo* means old; and *Viña* is vineyard.

Ribera del Duero

Ribera del Duero, located north of Madrid, is Spain's new, up-and-coming wine region. Until recently, the legendary Vega Sicilia winery dominated the region and its acclaim as producer of Spain's single most renowned wine, Unico (made mainly from Tempranillo, with some Cabernet Sauvignon). Unico is an intense, tannic, and concentrated red wine that requires long aging after its 10 years in cask, and several more years in bottle at the winery. It sells for more than $100 per bottle.

Rueda—Home of Verdejo

Located west of Ribera del Duero, the Rueda region is known for one of Spain's best white wines. Made from the Verdejo grape, which is slightly sweet and round on the palate, the wine is stylish with a fruity character. The price is attractive: from $6 to $8 per bottle.

Galicia

Galicia, on the Atlantic coast in northwest Spain, has one specific district, Rias Baixas, that boasts an exhilarating new wine: the white Albarino. This wine displays an intense acidity, flowery scents, and delicate flavors reminiscent of a Condrieu from France's Rhône Valley (see Chapter 7). Albarinos cost from about $8 to $17 per bottle.

Jerez de la Frontera—Sherry Anyone?

Jerez is a large wine region in southern Spain and is famous for the production of Sherry. The wines from Jerez are subject to the country's highest regulatory standards. The predominant grape here is the Palomino, a delicious variety, which undergoes a unique process to produce the fortified Sherry.

Sherry is produced in large volume by modern, efficient methods of crushing and vinification. The making of Sherry bears a definitive statement on the importance of soil as well as climate. As a viticultural area, Jerez is divided into three sections, all based on soil type:

Albariza   The most prized, and least productive, regions are characterized by *albariza*, a soil that is predominately chalk with parts of limestone and magnesium.

Barro   Another soil division, *barro* (literally "clay") is more productive.

Arena   The third region, *arena* (which means "sand"), bears vines that are immensely productive but weak in character.

Albariza, easy to recognize by the white top soils, bears the best Sherry grapes. By law, at least 40 percent of the grapes used in Sherry must come from albariza soils.

Portugal

If you grew up in the 1970s, there's a good chance your first wine was either Mateus or Lancer's. (Remember those strange-looking bottles?) These medium-dry and somewhat effervescent rosés are two of Portugal's most familiar wines. Perhaps its most famous wine is the dark dessert wine, Port, although more Americans have probably heard of it than experienced an authentic one.

Most Portuguese drink red and white table wines, which are less well known outside their own country. This lack of recognition should soon begin to change: The current trend toward modernization and stronger quality control should ensure Portugal higher status and visibility in the expanding world wine market.

The following are the tiers within the Portuguese classification system:

➤ **Denominação de Origem Controlada (DOC)**   The highest tier, it's awarded to only 11 wine regions.

Wine Word

Here are a few terms to help you learn about Portuguese wines: *Quinta* means estate or vineyard; *Colheita* is vintage year; *Seco* is dry; *Tinto* is red; and *Adega* means winery.

➤ **Indicação de Proveniencia Regulamentad (IPR)** The next tier, it has been awarded to 32 regions, many of which are waiting for elevation to DOC status. IPR corresponds roughly to the VDQS status of France.

➤ **Vinho de Mesa Regional** The Portuguese table wine category corresponds to the Spanish Vino de la Tierra and the French Vins de Pays.

➤ **Vinho de Mesa** This tier accounts for all remaining wines.

Port has its own system of classification, implemented and enforced by the rigid *Instituto do Vinho do Porto*. The appellation system for Port is called the *Denominação de Origem*, and follows stringent standards.

Vinho Verde—Do You Like Your Wine "Green"?

The color refers to the grapes, not the wine. This DOC region, between the Minhos and Douros Rivers, is the country's largest wine-producing region. Vinho Verdes (*vinho* means wine, and *verde* means green) are fresh, fruity wines made for early consumption. Their tart, bracing, refreshing character is enhanced by a distinct degree of effervescence. As the name suggests, the wines are acidic and have a pleasantly underripe character. White Vinho Verde wines can add a unique flair to your favorite seafood dish, and as for red Vinho Verdes (yes, there are red Vinho Verdes), well, let's just say they're definitely an acquired taste; the description "acidic" would be an understatement.

Wines of Portugal.

The most widely available Vinho Verdes are the brands Aveleda and Casal Garcia, which sell for $6 to $7 a bottle. These wines are medium dry, meant to be served chilled, and usually no more than ordinary. More expensive Vinho Verdes are made from the Alvarhino grape from the sub-region of Monção and retail for $12 to $20 per bottle. The higher quality Vinho Verdes are more complex, with some potential for aging. They may be hard to find but are worth the effort.

Dao—Affordable Table Wines

Dao is the country's finest table wine region. The best Dao wines are the reds, although there are also some quality whites. Most wines are blends from within the region, and some are vintage-dated. Those that are aged in wood casks are entitled to *Reserva* status (for vintage wines of superior quality); cask-aging makes them soft and mellow. Dao reds are typically smooth and full-bodied, while the whites are light and simple. Few stand out as distinctive, but they offer pleasant drinking at equally pleasant prices.

> ### Wine Word
>
> If you see the term *Garrafeira* on a bottle of red wine, it means the wine has been aged at least two years in cask and one year in bottle; on a bottle of white, it means the wine has been in cask and in bottle each for six months.

Douro—Home of Port

Located in northeastern Portugal, the Douro River region produces Portugal's most renowned wine, Port, along with sturdy red table wines. The steep and hilly terrain, with hot summers moderated by cool evenings, is ideal for growing the deep-colored, full-flavored grape varieties needed for Port. Some interesting table wines are also made from the local grapes; these wines are intense and robust and require years of aging.

Moscatel de Setubal

The excellent fortified sweet wines of this region still suffer the stigma of an erroneous and unfortunate association with the inferior, American-made Muscatel. They are both fortified wines—but the resemblance ends there. Setubal wines are deeply colored with a strong, complex Muscat character; they improve with long aging. Interestingly, the producers usually offer a six-year-old and a 25-year-old bottling. They are available here in fine wine stores, often at an attractive price for a wine of this high quality.

Chile—Spanish Roots, New World Flavor

Chilean winemaking is a cosmopolitan affair, with Italian, Spanish, French, and German influences. This process is particularly interesting for a country that's relatively isolated—bordered on one side by the lofty peaks of the Andes and on the other by the Pacific Ocean. The high coastal ranges protect much of the growing land from excess humidity, and the soothing Pacific protects it from excess heat.

Like California wines, Chilean wines carry varietal names, usually in conjunction with the region and sometimes the district. Many of Chile's white wines resemble inexpensive magnum wines from California. The reds are better and offer excellent value, ranging in price from $4 to $12 per bottle. Only since the mid-1980s has winemaking for export become a serious industry in Chile, and Chilean reds are not yet contenders in the arena of world-class wines. They do have potential, though; take, for example, the outstanding Don Melchor made from Cabernet Sauvignon by Concha y Toro, a winery known for its excellent, inexpensive varietal wines. The Chilean wine industry is constantly moving toward producing better varietal wines, and in a decade or so, should be a factor in world-class wines.

Chapter 10

Starring...Germany (and the rest of Europe)

AUF WHAT? | I DON'T KNOW.

In This Chapter

➤ The many wines of Germany

➤ Austrian wine

➤ The wines of Switzerland

➤ Greek wine

The wines of Germany offer a wide range of delightful experiences, but you must memorize, memorize, and memorize to be fully knowledgeable on the topic. Austrian wines are similar in style to German wines, but don't achieve the quality of the best German examples. The wines of Switzerland offer a unique style and taste. The wines of Greece offer simple inexpensive wines, delightful for everyday drinking. In this chapter we'll explore all these wine regions.

Germany—Zum Wohl! (Cheers!)

If you've ever tasted a German red, chances are you weren't too far from the banks of the Rhine—virtually no German red wines are exported. All the German wines you'll see in your favorite wine shop are white, but contrary to legend, not all are sweet. Some carry the word *Tröcken* on the label, which means dry. They do tend to be medium-dry to sweet, floral and fragrant, refreshing, and characteristically un-oaked.

The finest wine regions of Germany.

When reading a German wine label, always look for a varietal name along with the place. And don't be too complacent about how well you've gotten to understand the French AOC classification system. German wines require even more memorization. Since 1971, when German wine regulations were revised, the rules have become even stricter than those of France.

Where Riesling Reigns

Germany is the first home of the noble Riesling, a temperamental vinifera that ripens consistently only in Germany's best vineyards; because of its fussiness, Riesling grapes represent only 21 percent of all viticultural plantings. The most prolific grape variety is Müller-Thurgau, which ripens earlier than Riesling, and yields a soft, round, fragrant wine. It's not in the same class as Riesling, but because Müller-Thurgau loves the cool German climate, it's loved in return by the winegrowers. Other important white varietals include Sylvaner, Kerner, Scheurebe, and Ruländer (Pinot Gris). The red varietal Spatburgunder (Pinot Noir) is grown in the warmer parts of the country.

German Wine Laws Simplified

Germany is the only country where you can judge a wine's quality by how long it takes you to read the label. German wines, like many other European wines, are first named for their place of origin, which is usually a village name and a vineyard name—for example, Bernkasteler Graben (town, vineyard). Add to this the name of the varietal: *Bernkasteler Graben Riesling*. Finally, add the *Prädikat* (a term that describes the ripeness of the grapes): *Bernkasteler Graben Riesling Spätlese*. Wines that are given a Prädikat constitute the highest tier in the German classification system and represent the highest quality wines.

The system of assigning rank to ripeness is not so unusual when you consider the cool climate in Germany, where ripeness is the desired, but sometimes elusive, goal. There are five Prädikat levels. Following is a list of the levels, from the lowest to the highest (ripest):

➤ *Kabinett*

➤ *Spätlese*

➤ *Auslese*

➤ *Beerenauslese*

➤ *Tröckenbeerenauslese*

The finest wines at each level are made from the Riesling grape, though the quality of wines made from other grape varieties improves with the ripeness of the grape. Kabinett wines are generally relatively dry, fruity, and well balanced. Spätlese wines are made from grapes ranging from fairly ripe to greatly mature, and can span the spectrum from fairly dry to slightly sweet. For Auslese, Beerenauslese, and Tröckenbeerenauslese wines, see the section "Sweet and Late-Harvest Wines" later in this chapter.

German wines also fall into one of three tiers:

➤ **Qualitätswein mit Prädikat (QmP)**   The highest tier, it means *quality wines with a special attribute*; wines with a ripeness rating are in this category.

➤ **Qualitätswein bestimmter Anbaugebiet (QbA)**   Also called simply *Qualitätswein*, the title of this second tier means *quality wines from a special region*.

➤ **Tafelwien or Landwein**   *Table wine* (or wine with a regional indicator) makes up the lowest tier; fewer than 10 percent of German wines fall into this category.

Wine regulations also define viticultural areas as follows:

➤ *Bereich* is a large, wine-growing region, and may be subdivided into one or more Grosslage.

➤ *Grosslage* means large site. It's essentially a large vineyard that contains smaller vineyards

(*Enzillagen*)—sometimes several hundred acres and thousands of vineyards, all of which produce wines of similar quality and character. A wine from a Grosslage is identified on the label with a generic name that reads like a vineyard name. The only way to tell the difference is to memorize the *Grosslagen* names.

➤ *Einzellage* is the smallest defined region, an individual vineyard that contains at least 12 acres. The Enzellage is indicated on the label after the village name.

Wine Wisdom

In addition to indicating the region, place, varietal, and sometimes ripeness, each bottle of German wine carries a *control number* specifying the year of production, the year of registration, and a code number identifying the producer and the individual lot of wine.

What Is Liebfraumilch?

Liebfraumilch, which translates as "milk of the Virgin," is a delightful, refreshing, enjoyable wine. Who can dislike a wine with a name like that? Actually, the wine's name comes from its origin in a vineyard surrounding a church dedicated to Our Lady, located in Worms in the Rheinhessen region. Liebfraumilch is probably the best known German wine in the Untied States, and is, for many people, their first taste of *vitis vinifera*.

Yellow in color, with a slight greenish hue, Liebfraumilch is a blend of several grape varieties, primarily Müller-Thurgau with Riesling, Sylvaner, and/or Kerner. It's mainly produced in the Rheinhessen and Pfalz regions (the two main regions), and is ranked QbA. Typically low in alcohol, it is medium-dry, with a refreshing acidity, and a pleasant fruity flavor, and is definitely meant to be enjoyed young. Liebfraumilch sells for $5 to $7 per bottle.

Tröcken Wines

Outside of Germany, many people are familiar only with *lieblich* (gentle) wines, which are fruity, light-bodied, and pleasingly sweet. But there are other styles, less sweet, that have become trendy in the German homeland. The driest category is *tröcken* (dry). Tröcken wines have virtually no residual sugar and range in taste from austere to tart. *Halbtröcken* (half-dry) wines are midway between tröcken and lieblich. More mellow than tröcken wines, they have a certain amount of residual sugar and a fairly dry taste. They are somewhat higher in alcohol than Kabinett or Spätlese wines.

Sweet and Late-Harvest Wines

This category contains the wines from the Auslese category on up. They're made from grapes that are over-ripened, rot-infected, or frozen—but who's to argue with success? These are some of the world's finest and most unique wines.

> ➤ **Auslese**   These wines are made from overripe grapes, which endow the wine with a fuller body and a higher concentration of flavor. Their sweetness is usually balanced by sufficient acidity.

> ➤ **Beerenauslese**   These wines are made from over-ripe grapes that have usually been attacked by the noble rot, *Botrytis*, which gives them a honeyed and luscious opulence. Winemakers choosing to make a Beerenauslese are gamblers: They risk losing their

crop to frost as the grapes are left on the vine to ripen. As a result, only a small quantity of Beerenauslese is produced every year, and it's appropriately expensive.

➤ **Tröckenbeerenauslese** These are the most exotic wines in the hierarchy. The individually selected berries are usually attacked by *Botrytis* (although it's not a legal requirement), and the resulting wines possess a concentrated lusciousness, like nectar—no doubt this is the beverage the gods enjoy in Valhalla. This wine is a killer to make. It's not only risky, but it's a difficult wine to vinify and requires superior skill, dedication, and TLC throughout the winemaking process. Prices can easily reach the three-figure range for a halb-bottle.

➤ **Eiswein** Literally, "ice wine," Eiswein is made from grapes left on the vine to freeze (talk about turning a liability into an asset!). Once harvested, the grapes are crushed gently to retain the grape juice but not the ice. The juice left to undergo fermentation is richly concentrated in sugar, flavor, and acidity. Depending on the skill of the winemaker, this opulent wine can equal the finest Auslese, Beerenaulese, or Tröckenbeerenauslese.

The Home of the Rhine Maidens

Four of Germany's wine regions bear the name of the renowned river: Rheingau, Rheinhessen, Pfalz (formerly called the Rheinphalz), and Mittelrhein.

Rheingau

The Rheingau is a tiny wine region, but along with the Mosel-Saar-Ruwer, it is the most important in Germany. It's divided into 10 Grosslagen and 120 Einzellagen over 28 communities perched along the banks of the Rhine. Riesling grapes account for more than 80 percent of the vineyard planting and produce the finest wines of the region. The Rieslings tend to be round, soft, and deep in color. The leading Grosslagen of the Rheingau are as follows (in parentheses are the most notable Einzellagen):

➤ Hochheim (Domdechaney, Hölle, Sommerheil, Schloss Eltz, Taubenberg, and Sonnenberg)

➤ Erbach (Marcobrunn)

➤ Hattenheim (Steinberg)

➤ Winkle (Schloss Vollrads)

➤ Rauenthaler (Baiken, Wülfen, Langenstrück, and Nonnenburg)

➤ Eltville

➤ Johannisberg (Schloss Johannisberg)

Rheinhessen

The large Rheinhessen region produces a greater variety of wines than any other German wine district. Rheinhessen wines account for 50 percent of all German wine exports; the most famous export is Liebfraumilch, which is made by nearly 99 percent of the region's 167 villages.

Wine Wisdom

The best Rheinhessen wines are the long-lived Rieslings from the region of *Nierstein*. Other good ones come from the vineyards of *Bingen*, *Nachenheim*, and *Wonnegau*.

Rheinhessen wines tend to be soft, with a pronounced character that makes them the easiest to identify of all German wines. The popularity of the Rheinhessen wines is probably based on their intense bouquet and straight-forward sweetness. Most Rheinhessen wines are made from the Müller-Thurgau grape, which produces juicy, soft, fruity wines. The next most widely used vine is the Sylvaner, which produces full, round wines.

The Pfalz

The Pfalz region is close in size to the Rheinhessen. In its finer vineyards, the soil contains large amounts of *Schist* (slate), which retains heat during the cool evening hours. A long, warm fall fosters grape maturity and enables the area to produce intense, sweet wines ranging from Spätlese to Tröckenbeerenauslese. This region also produces some of the world's finest Auslese and Beerenauslese wines. Some of these high-ranked Prädikat achieve super-premium or noble status.

The predominant grape is the Müller-Thurgau, which yields pale, fresh wines. As in other areas, the finest wines come from the noble Riesling, which accounts for only 14 percent of all vineyard plantings. Pfalz Rieslings offer an attractive and remarkable balance: They're fuller than those of the Mosel (which we'll get to soon), less mild and less soft than those of the Rheinhessen, and less overwhelming in bouquet than those of the Rheingau. In general, wines of the Pfalz tend to have more body and an earthier character than the wines of the Rheingau. The best Pfalz wines are produced by **Forst**, **Diedesheim**, **Ruppertsberg**, and **Wachenheim**.

The Mosel

The region composed of the vineyards dotting the slopes of the serpentine Mosel and its tributaries, the Saar and Ruwer, has come to be known as the Mosel-Saar-Ruwer. Divided in two, the area is comprised of the Mittelmosel (Central Mosel), which produces the greatest wines of the region, and the Saar-Ruwer, which produces good, though not necessarily distinctive, wines.

Wine Wisdom

You can easily tell a Mosel wine by the color of its bottle. It's green—the rest of Germany uses brown bottles.

About 55 percent of the plantings in the Mosel are Riesling. Mosel Rieslings are light in body, delicate, and refined. They are often described as floral wines, evoking images of colorful, blooming spring meadows. They have a lively and refreshing taste, are low in alcohol, and often contain a slight effervescence. These wines are meant to be drunk young.

The Bereich **Bernkastel** is the best known in the Mittelmosel, and premium and noble wines are produced by four of its six Grosslagen (the two others, Probstberg and St. Michael, produce simple-premium wines):

➤ **Michelsberg**   The best wines come from the village of Piesport (the wines are called Piesporter Michaelberg); also notable are Trittneheim and Neumagen.

➤ **Kurfürstlay**   The two best wine-producing villages are Brauneberg (where the best vineyard is Juffer) and Bernkastle (where the celebrated Dokter property produces extraordinary noble wines).

➤ **Münzlay**   The villages of Graach, Wehlen, and Zeltingen yield wines that can achieve super-premium or noble status.

➤ **Scharzberg**   Wine quality varies greatly here along the Saar River, but the noble wine of the region is Scharzhofberger, followed by wines from Ockfen, Oberemmel, and Ayl.

Austria—From the Vienna Woods

Austria produces three times as much wine as Switzerland, and like Switzerland, it enjoys its own beverage: Annual per capita wine consumption is roughly 10 gallons. Interestingly, none of the country's wine comes from the regions that border Germany, Italy, or Switzerland. Baden, near Vienna, produces light, fruity-style wines, and the best wines of Austria come from the three eastern provinces:

➤ Langenlois

➤ Krems

➤ Wachau

Most of Austria's red wine is produced in Burgenland, one of the country's warmer regions, which borders Hungary. The red wines are medium- to full-bodied, with a fruity character and moderate tannins. Eighty percent of Austrian wines are white. The most popular wines are made from the indigenous white Gruner Veltliner. Its wines are full-bodied and refreshing, with herbal and, occasionally, vegetal flavors. Müller-Thurgau is widely planted, along with Welschriesling, a grape frequently used to make ordinary table wines in Eastern Europe. It excels in quality in Austria and tends to be light, soft, and aromatic. Sylvaner, Riesling, and Ruländer (Pinot Gris) are also planted here, and these wines are similar in style to German wines. They rarely reach the same heights, but Austria's sweet late-picked, berry-selected, and dessert-style wines have received international acclaim.

Austrian wine laws follow the German model. Better wines are divided into *Qualitätswein* and *Prädikatswein* classifications; in Austria, however, the Prädikat rankings begin with Spätlese. The minimum ripeness required for each level is higher in Austria than in Germany, and Austrian wines are typically higher in alcohol. The German system of labeling also applies to Austrian wines: The place name and varietal name are usually linked, but there are a few exceptions, such as in Burgenland, where wines generally carry varietal names followed by the region name.

Switzerland—Keeping the Good Things for Themselves

Switzerland enjoys its wines; its unusually high annual wine consumption is close to 12 gallons per capita. Unfortunately for the rest of the wine world, the Swiss enjoy their wines so much that they keep most of them at home.

The canton of Vaud is the largest wine-growing region, followed by the Valais to the south. Like Germany, roughly two-thirds of Switzerland's wines are white. Swiss wines tend to be expensive for their quality and, therefore, aren't really good values. They are, however, interesting wines with a character all their own.

Vaud

Most of the vineyards here are located on the slopes surrounding beautiful Lake Geneva (Lac Léman). The two major sub-regions are Laveaux and La Côte. (Guess what language they speak here?) Laveaux is on the south shore of the lake, and La Côte is on the north shore. The predominant grape variety is the Chasselas, which yields a grapy, if neutral, white wine; these wines are also fairly full-bodied and dry, with straightforward earthy flavors.

Valais

The Valais has a few warmer growing sites, particularly on the slopes near the Rhône River. The Müller-Thurgau grape is called Johannisberg here, and Chasselas is known by its local name, Fendant; in this temperate climate, Chasselas develops full-bodied, well-balanced wines. The local red wine, called Dôle, is made from either Gamay or

Pinot Noir (also known as Petit-Dôle) grapes. The Pinot Gris grape produces Malvoisie, a soft, sweet, dessert-style wine. Some local wines to try include Arvine, Amirgne, Humagne, and Rèze.

Wine Wisdom

In case you manage to find a Swiss wine in your favorite wine shop (or you're planning a holiday on Lake Geneva or in the Alps), here's a tip for reading Swiss wine labels: Most Swiss wines carry a place name, often with the name of a grape variety, and a town name.

Neuchâtel

The region of Neuchâtel in the northwest corner of Switzerland produces quality red and white table wines—an unusual feat this far north. Remarkably, the fussy Pinot Noir yields a delicate, fruity style of wine; the better, light wines come from the village of Cortaillod.

Ticino

Ticino is located in Italian Switzerland, in the country's southern corner. Most of the vineyards here are planted in red varieties. Nostrano is the name for a light, blended red. Viti is the name for fuller-bodied reds made from Merlot.

Greece—Where the Bacchae Reveled

Greece, the birthplace of the god of wine Dionysus, is one of the world's oldest wine-growing regions. Attica, the home of the Parthenon, is one of the principle wine-producing areas, and is where most of retsina (a white wine flavored with resin) is made. The largest wine district, the Peloponnese produces predominately sweet wines; other local wines flow freely from many of the isles: Crete, Samos, Santorini, Rhodes, and Corfu. Little is exported to the United States, but if you're planning a trip, there's plenty of it waiting.

Wine Wisdom

A few pleasant, fruity red and white table wines are exported from Greece to the United States. They're very drinkable and relatively inexpensive. The largest producers are Achaia-Clauss and Andrew Cambas. For quality wines, you generally can't go wrong with Boutari.

Fortified dessert wines are the second most important type of Greek wine. First in prestige is the dark red Mavrodaphne, which is similar to but lower in alcohol content than California Port.

The New World

Winemaking in America is a relatively new industry; it didn't become a full-scale growth industry in California until the 1970s. Today, there are more than 600 wineries in California—most are small, but they're growing in both quantity and quality. Unlike most wine-producing regions, grape growers and winemakers in California are often two different animals. Grapes may be grown by ranchers in one area and sent off to a winery in another. Or a winery may grow its own grapes in numerous different regions throughout the state. When it comes to wine in America, and in California in particular, reading the wine label is of utmost importance: Because of wine regulations without teeth, information on the label is often misleading and may not be an indication of quality. This chapter introduces you to the ins and outs of choosing an American-made wine.

American Wine Laws

Yes, we do have them, but sad to say, U.S. regulations offer consumers the least amount of quality protection of any major wine-producing country. American wine laws don't dictate the quality of the wine produced in its appellations: A region, like Napa, California, may produce some of the finest wine in the country as well as some of the poorest, while using the same appellations. To buy American wine, you must know your producers.

As for those wine laws, the U.S. does have an appellation system that designates the regions where wine is produced: the *American Viticultural Areas* (AVAs). Unfortunately, the regulations don't extend any further. The United States has no regulations regarding which grape varieties can be planted where, or the maximum yield of grapes per acre. In addition, there are AVAs within AVAs, adding to the confusion. The end result for the consumer is that very little on American wine labels will help him or her to differentiate a quality wine from an ordinary wine. Many people figure if it has a varietal name, and it doesn't have a screw cap, it must be a quality wine. They're often sadly disappointed.

American wines are only required to state bare essentials on the label. Wines carrying a varietal name have to be made from at least 75 percent of the designated grape, but these wines can still be mass produced, and consequently be of mediocre quality. An AVA indication means at least 85 percent of the grapes must come from the named AVA, but that particular AVA could include areas that produce only mediocre wine as well as areas that produce the finest (such as Napa Valley, California).

When the state designation on the bottle is California, 100 percent of the grapes used have to be grown within California. Other states require only 75 percent to be grown in-state. The following are a few more terms that you'll see on wine bottles:

➤ *Estate bottled* or *Grown, produced, and bottled by* means that 100 percent of the grapes were either grown or controlled by the vintner and that he made all the wine. The problem is that even the cheapest and most mediocre wine can be "Estate bottled," so this term is often meaningless.

➤ *Produced and bottled by* means that the named winery made and bottled at least 75 percent of the wine in the bottle.

➤ *Made and bottled by* means that the named winery made at least 10 percent of the wine. (Pretty big difference, isn't there?)

➤ A vintage date on the bottle means that at least 95 percent of the wine was made from grapes grown and fermented during that year.

➤ *Reserve*, *Special Reserve*, and *Vintner's Reserve* don't really mean anything at all: There are no regulations regarding these terms, and wineries often use them on its lesser wines to promote sales. (Meanwhile, its better wines are bottled without any special attributes indicated.) Quite a marketing ploy!

It's all very confusing, and it's a shame that the U.S. government didn't adopt the kind of meaningful regulations found elsewhere in the winemaking community.

Navigating the California Wine Maze

Unlike France, where each region specializes in a particular kind of wine or wine made from only one or a few grape varieties, in the United States you will find that most grape varieties are grown in AVAs. Some grapes excel in certain areas and do poorly in others. In a case where the grape does not create great wine, you are paying for a grape grower's experiment in planting varietal wines. The following sections describe the California AVAs (appellations).

The best-known wine regions of California.

Appellation California

This is one of those huge regional categories—it's the broadest tier on the label, and it means that the wine comes from anywhere within the Golden State. California alone requires that the bottles contain 100 percent home-grown grapes. Wines from this broad appellation generally range from ordinary everyday to simple-premium quality.

Appellation North Coast

This appellation restricts the growing area to one of the better winegrowing regions within the state. Wines in this category begin in the everyday range and go up to mid-premium quality. The North Coast AVA contains the following:

➤ Napa Valley

➤ Sonoma Valley

➤ Mendocino County

➤ Lake County

Central Valley—Home of Inexpensive Wine

This hot, sun-drenched region, approximately 100 miles long, produces high-yielding grape varieties used to make the majority of bulk wine that goes into blended, jug, or everyday wines. That said, some producers, such as Robert Mondavi (known for his high-quality Napa Cabernets), have begun to grow better varietals in the Lodi area; these wines, sold in magnums at relatively low prices, make fine everyday wines.

Top California Wine Regions

California has no less than 13 highly ranked wine-producing regions, some of which have AVAs within their AVA. Each one has its own distinctive style and its preferred grape varieties. The regions range in character from glamorous and palatial Napa Valley to scenic, seaside Monterey (the charming village that has become a hub of technology and innovation). Californians do everything in a big way.

Napa Valley—The Hollywood of Vines

Napa Valley is sort of the Bordeaux of California—whether this reputation is warranted is another matter, as some pretty mediocre wines are produced here along with some of the finest. Regardless, the region, lying northeast of San Francisco, is unquestionably beautiful; it's a major Bay Area tourist attraction, and even has its own tourist railroad. Vineyard land here is at a premium; more than 200 wineries are tightly packed into a relatively small growing space.

Grape Alert

To many people, a Napa Valley appellation on a wine label equals immediate prestige. In reality, Napa wines range from ordinary to sublime, and to figure out which wines fall into the latter category, you'll have to study your wineries.

Within the broad Napa Valley appellation are eight AVAs, not including the Carneros AVA (which we'll get to soon), which is shared by Napa and Sonoma valleys. These are the eight AVAs:

➤ Spring Mountain

➤ Mt. Veeder

➤ Howell Mountain

➤ Stags Leap District

➤ Atlas Peak

➤ Wild Horse Valley

➤ Rutherford

➤ Oakville

The white varietal name most closely associated with Napa is Chardonnay. The finest quality have a ripe aroma and flavor that is frequently spicy, with a melange of apricot, pineapple, and citrus flavors. The texture is rich and luscious, and the alcohol levels are high—13 percent or more—giving the wines a headiness when young. Some are fermented in oak barrels in the true Burgundian fashion, or aged in small French oak casks. This regimen endows the Chardonnays with a vanilla character that harmonizes with its varietal personality, as well as a bit of oaky bitterness. Mid-premium Napa Chardonnays are made from less-ripe grapes and/or spend less time aging in those small barrels. They are fruity, appley, and less complex.

Napa's second most celebrated varietal is another white, Sauvignon Blanc (also called Fumé Blanc). The best of these are made in a style resembling their French counterparts. They rarely rival the finest Sauvignon Blanc of the Graves or the Médoc—but then, neither do most of the Sauvignon grown in France. Napa Valley Sauvignon Blancs range from subtle, light, and moderately oaked to heavy, powerful, warm, and very oaky. It all depends on the winery's style. Most of them fall into the mid-premium category. In general, Napa style leans toward full ripeness in the grapes, producing wines with high alcohol, which are counterbalanced with assertive oak flavors that mingle with the grape's personality. Age is no matter; they're attractive when young and are capable of good bottle aging.

Napa is not too well known for its Rieslings (usually labeled *Johannisberg Riesling*), but some of its finest Late Harvest wines can stand up to the most noble of Germany's Rieslings. Some vineyards in Napa (along with Sonoma and Monterey counties) will regularly develop *botrytis*, which allows for the production of Late Harvest wines in the German tradition. Because there is no U.S. equivalent to the German *pradikat*, you have to look for the term *Late*

Harvest on the label. It may also state the percentage of residual sugar. These Late Harvest wines can achieve super-premium or even noble status. They offer the floral Riesling character, along with *botrytis* complexity—honeyed aroma, and a hint of almonds with corresponding acid balance to parallel the sweetness. In some instances, it's hard to tell the difference between these wines and their German prototypes.

Few dry or slightly sweet Napa Rieslings can match the unique style and charm of their counterparts from the Rhine and Mosel, but they can equal Rieslings from anywhere else in the world. They tend to be fuller in body, particularly in middle body, and more fruity than the German versions.

Wine Wisdom

Bordeaux-style blended wines have appeared in greater numbers during the past decade. The reds are usually made from red Bordeaux varieties: *Cabernet Sauvignon*, *Cabernet Franc*, *Merlot*, and sometimes *Malbec* and *Petit Verdot*. The whites are usually made from the white Bordeaux grapes *Sauvignon Blanc* and *Semillon*.

Now the reds.

Napa Valley Cabernet Sauvignon ranks among California's best—when it's made to be the best. Wines from a select few from sites in the Rutherford, Oakville, and Stags Leap districts can achieve noble status. Well-made Napa Cabernets offer a berryish, herbal aroma, fairly full body, ample tannins, and some warmth. The super-premiums have a riper character, reminiscent of cassis, dried sage, and black currants, that often develops a cedary "cigar-box" characteristic with bottle aging. The best of these will benefit from aging for a decade or more.

Merlot is rapidly gaining in stature and popularity. It's easier than Cabernet Sauvignon to enjoy: Its tannins are less harsh and less astringent than those of Cabernet. Napa has the edge on quality Merlots. The best are very ripe and herbaceous in aroma and flavor. They have a round, soft, and voluptuous character, and you'll frequently notice a somewhat sweet finish.

Super-premium Napa Valley Zinfandels come from hill-sides or very old vineyards. Zinfandel reigns in the Calistoga region, the area's warmest sub-region. Most Zinfandels are berrylike and medium-bodied, with moderate tannins and a tart finish. That's red Zinfandel we're talking about. The blush wine, white Zinfandel, which has recently soared to popularity, is light, sweet, and fruity—good for summer and leisurely drinking.

Sonoma—No Glitter, Just Good Wine

Although it's home to some of California's best wineries, the Sonoma wine-growing region lacks the lavish estates that characterize Napa Valley. It may not be prime on the tourist map, but it's certainly a hot spot on the wine map.

To make things just a bit more confusing with the AVAs-within-AVAs business, Sonoma County has two broader AVAs: Northern Sonoma, a somewhat scattered designation encompassing the Russian River Valley, Alexander Valley, Dry Creek Valley, and Knight's Valley; and Sonoma Coast, which contains a mélange of land situated along the coast in western Sonoma. The following are the designated AVAs of Sonoma:

➤ Sonoma Valley

➤ Sonoma Mountain

➤ Dry Creek Valley

➤ Alexander Valley

➤ Russian River Valley

➤ Sonoma-Green Valley (contained within Russian River Valley)

➤ Chalk Hill (also contained within Russian River Valley)

➤ Knights Valley

The Dry Creek appellation of Sonoma deserves special mention. Dry Creek is celebrated for its Chardonnays, Sauvignon Blancs, Cabernet Sauvignons, and Zinfandels. In fact, it's a Zinfandel haven: The super-premium Dry Creek red Zinfandels have an earthy, peppery character, and a richness and depth that distinguish it from other Zinfandels. Alexander Valley also produces fine Zinfandels of mid- to super-premium quality; these offer a distinct, ripe cherry, blackberry character.

Some mid- and super-premium quality Chardonnays come from Sonoma; these tend to be fruitier and leaner than Napa's and are improved by long bottle aging. Along with the Dry Creek district, the Alexander Valley district tends to accentuate a very fruity varietal aroma with a lemony flavor; these wines have a medium-bodied, slightly viscous texture. Only the Dry Creek district is noted for its Sauvignon Blancs.

Only a few California wineries have managed to handle the finicky Pinot Noir, and some of the best are in Sonoma, particularly in the Russian River Valley. They offer the characteristic Pinot Noir fruitiness, a slightly cherry, smoky character, medium body, and slight tannins. Making a great Pinot Noir in California has been the result of continuing experimentation.

Wine Wisdom

Although many California wines are meant to be consumed when bottled, the super-premium and noble quality wines benefit from bottle aging. Chardonnay will benefit from two to four years of aging. Reds such as Cabernet Sauvignon, Merlot, and the better Zinfandels can benefit from upwards of five to 10 years of aging.

Sonoma is also home to many mid-premium Cabernet Sauvignons. Most are vinous and straightforward, medium-bodied, moderately tannic, and early maturing, with a slightly weedy, peppery character. These traits are especially evident in wines from Dry Creek, Alexander Valley, and the Sonoma Valley.

Carneros—Numero Uno

Carneros is the single most important wine growing district in California. Extending from the southern part of Napa Valley into Sonoma County, it enjoys the cool breezes from the Pacific and the mists rolling in from San Pablo Bay. Carneros is home to grapes that thrive in a cool climate and are used for high-quality sparkling wines: Chardonnay, Pinot Noir, and various white varieties.

The winemakers of Carneros have managed to tame the Pinot Noir grape, creating some mid- to super-premium wines. The Pinots are typically deep colored with herbal, cherryish, and slightly roasted aromas and flavors, a velvety texture, some depth, and a long finish.

Stags Leap—Cabernet Country

Stags Leap in Napa is celebrated for its outstanding Cabernet Sauvignon. (For characteristics, see Napa varietals.)

Monterey—Charm and Ingenuity

Monterey is a microcosm of California viticulture—a synthesis of experimentation and technology. The growers and winemakers have triumphed over such pitfalls as vegetative Cabernets (in the early 1970s they tasted like uncooked asparagus and smelled like bell peppers), and that nasty little bug, phylloxera. In true California spirit, the winemakers—and the wine—survived and thrived.

Drawing on the techniques of Burgundy winemaking, Monterey Chardonnay has been coaxed into full potential. Monterey Chardonnays tend to have more varietal character in aroma and flavor than their counterparts produced farther north. They possess depth, texture, and astringency; the accent is on fresh, varietal fruitiness. Many Monterey-grown Chardonnays have a unique green or grassy character, medium body, and a sharp, crisp finish. Small-barrel oak aging is the method of choice to soften the wine's sharp edges.

Monterey is also one of the best California regions for Sauvignon Blanc. At mid-premium quality status, these wines yield a characteristic grassy, weedy, or black-pepper flavor. The region's dry or slightly sweet Rieslings are flowery yet firm; these "Soft Rieslings," which are similar to German Kabinett wines, are low in alcohol and meant for sipping. Monterey Gewürztraminers can be spicy in fragrance and fruity in flavor; some retain a slight Muscat character, and the best can improve with several years of bottle aging.

Monterey Cabernet Sauvignon has managed to shed its vegetable-garden image. Since the late 1970s, innovative winemakers have learned to cope with their unusual regional trait—and use it to advantage. The Cabernets have an herbal, spicy flavor; a moderate, peppery overtone; and good varietal character.

> **Wine Wisdom**
>
> The growing *Santa Cruz* wine region is home to some of the best wineries in California. The cool, breezy climate nurtures Pinot Noir, Cabernet Sauvignon, and Chardonnay. The appellation Santa Cruz appears on many big-styled, ripe Chardonnays and Pinot Noirs.

Amador County—Zinfandel Gold

Amador is located in the Sierra foothills where weary but hopeful prospectors once panned for gold. Few of them found it; the winegrowers who discovered the native Zinfandel did a lot better.

Zinfandel grapes reach full ripeness in this region, and the grapes are generally warm, fruity, and very tannic. Small amounts of Cabernet Sauvignon, Sauvignon Blanc, and Riesling are also grown and bottled here, but Zinfandel reigns supreme.

Santa Cruz—Rugged and Growing

Santa Cruz is a beautiful, mountainous area that runs from San Francisco south to the town of Santa Cruz. A decade ago, it was home to a dozen small wineries; today, the number is growing, and some of its wineries are the best in California. This is a cool growing region, with sea breezes on both sides. Pinot Noir grows happily on the Pacific side, while Cabernet Sauvignon prefers the San Francisco Bay area. Chardonnay likes them both (as do most tourists).

The appellation Santa Cruz appears on many big-styled, ripe Chardonnays and Pinot Noirs.

Santa Barbara County—A Proud Newcomer

Santa Barbara County, with its beautiful rolling hills, is a relative newcomer to the wine industry. The area is known mostly for wineries using the Santa Ynez appellation, although the Santa Maria and Los Alamos valleys are now gaining in stature.

Santa Barbara Chardonnays tend to be relatively early maturing; they have a unique grassiness and, depending on sugar development (which determines the alcoholic content), they range from very firm and hard in style to rounder and softer (although few have the rich texture that earmarks Napa Chardonnays). They also have excellent acidity and a slightly silky texture.

Some Sauvignon Blanc is produced in Santa Ynez. It tends to have an aggressive, pronounced aroma of grassiness, black pepper, and fruit that needs to be tamed and rounded by cask aging, bottle aging, or blending with a small percentage of Semillon. (In California, wines are often blended with grapes from other regions.)

Santa Barbara Cabernets have moderate, Bordeaux-like alcohol levels (under 13 percent), and a rich, herbal, berry-like aroma and flavor made complex by a weedy overtone, and—in some cases—by oakiness from long-aging in small casks. They tend to have a short finish when compared to the regal, lingering aftertaste found in the Cabernets of Napa and the middle Médoc of Bordeaux.

A good portion of Santa Barbara's growing wine reputation is founded on the affinity of the Pinot Noir grape for its soil and ocean air. The Pinots are often deep colored with herbal, cherryish, and slightly roasted aroma and flavors, a velvety texture, some depth, and a long finish.

The Golden State's Best Values

California's best values are found in the everyday and simple- to mid-premium wines that are produced in large quantities. California's best wines, the super-premium and noble wines, are produced in small quantities and are sought after by collectors who drive up the price beyond the wine's intrinsic value. At auction, these wines (with a few years behind them) bring astronomical prices. Here's a tip: Look to California for its lower-priced wines and to Bordeaux, Burgundy, Italy, and elsewhere for super-premium wines because they will provide comparable wines at lower prices.

The Pacific Northwest

North of California is a thriving wine industry, although Washington and Oregon are not exactly household words in the world of wine. The Cascade Mountains cut through both states, producing distinctive climatic regions and distinctive wines. In the following sections, I discuss the winemaking regions in the northwest United States.

Washington—North and Dry

Washington state began growing vinifera varieties in the 1960s, although few wineries actually existed until two decades later. Most of the vineyards are situated in the east, where rainfall is less prolific and the climate is continental (or even desert-like).

The winegrowing regions of Washington are as follows:

➤ **Yakima Valley** Located in southeast Washington, this area has cool summer weather, a long growing season, and 22 wineries.

➤ **Columbia** The largest of the Washington winegrowing regions, Columbia has 11 wineries; Puget Sound wineries often use Columbia grapes.

➤ **Walla Walla Valley** With only six wineries, this region accounts for less than one percent of the state's viticultural output.

Gewürztraminer and Johannisberg Riesling do well in Washington, growing with excellent varietal character and a less sweet style than their California cousins. Washington state Sauvignon Blancs are noted for their powerful character, while the ubiquitous Chardonnay is inconsistent in quality. Chenin Blanc, Cabernet Sauvignon, and Merlot round out Washington's most prolific varietals. The Washington-based Columbia Crest Merlot is currently the biggest-selling Merlot in the United States.

Oregon—Taming Pinot Noir

Oregon's main winegrowing region, Willamette Valley, encompasses a sizable area south of the city of Portland. This area is extremely cool during the summer and often quite rainy during the harvest season. Because Pinot Noir favors a cool climate, Oregon winemaking has made its name on this most finicky of grapes. Recently, Pinot Noir has been joined in Oregon by that other Pinot, Pinot Gris.

Warmer than Willamette—although still cool—the Umqua Valley is the home of Oregon's pioneering winery, Hillcrest Vineyards. Pinot Noir also thrives in Umpqua, along with Riesling (historically Oregon's second most important varietal), Chardonnay, and Cabernet Sauvignon. Hillcrest, which began Oregon's wine industry in 1962, is noted for its fine Rieslings.

The Rogue River Valley is a relative newcomer. It's the warmest of the Oregon growing regions, ideal for Cabernet Sauvignon and Merlot, as well as, of course, Chardonnay, which really took the advice, "Go West!" Pinot Gris is also beginning to make some inroads here.

New York State—Wine from Back East

Remember those "I Love New York" commercials? Do you recall seeing any wineries? They might have included the Brotherhood Winery in the Hudson Valley—founded in 1839; it's the oldest winery in operation anywhere in the United States. Or they might have shown the Canandaigua Wine Company in the Finger Lakes, the country's second largest winery. But they didn't. To most people, New York State is the home of New York City and Woodstock, and perhaps some nifty areas for hiking and climbing. Although New York is second in wine production to California, its reputation is vastly eclipsed by the Golden State.

Unlike California, New York's viticultural staple had always been *Vitus lambrusca*, great for jams, jellies, and unfermented beverages, but not so much for fine wines. New York winemakers have also had to deal with high production costs and labor-intensive means to protect their vines from the harsh, freezing winter. There's no soothing Pacific on this side of the country. Hence, except for low-priced champagne, the wines of New York cost more to make than their West Coast counterparts, and are consequently more costly in the store.

> ➤ **Finger Lakes**   The cold climate of the Finger Lakes district in western New York is somewhat tempered by the four large bodies of water. Approximately 85 percent of the state's wines come from this district. Riesling and Chardonnay are the two most successful varietals. During the 1980s, Finger Lakes wineries such as Glenora and Hermann J. Weimer began paving the way toward high-quality vinifera wines.

> ➤ **Long Island**   The North Fork AVA, 80 miles from New York City, has shown great promise with several vinifera grapes, notably Riesling, Pinot Noir, and Cabernet Sauvignon. Recently, Merlot and

Sauvignon Blanc have also been thriving. Long Island's second AVA consists of the Hamptons at the South Fork. The Hamptons is far more celebrated for its luxurious summer homes than its wine, and wines from these regions tend to be purchased by the trendy, who summer in the Hamptons.

➤ **Hudson River Valley** A mere 40 miles from New York City, the Hudson River Valley is home to Benmarl, Clinton, and several other wineries—including the historic Brotherhood, which caters to a tourist crowd. These wineries have shown good progress with better quality French hybrids and occasionally succeed with the vinifera grapes. The region also grows labrusca varieties, which are often sold to wineries in the Finger Lakes district.

Wines from Other States

Virtually every state within the viticultural temperature zone grows grapes and makes wine—from Idaho to Texas, from New Jersey to Virgina. Most of these wines are simple and not much to speak of, but they are interesting to try if you live in the locality where they are made. Besides, you'll be supporting a local winemaker, who probably needs it—such local winemaking ventures are rarely very lucrative. You may find the wines expensive for what's in the bottle, but when you're entertaining out-of-towners, the pride of serving a locally made wine more than makes up for the cost. Look for wineries in your locality and try their wares—you might be in for a pleasant surprise.

Chapter 12

Wine Bottle Secrets

At one time, the shape of a wine bottle provided a good indication of its contents. As bottles become more standardized, however, this indication becomes less apparent. Interestingly, the most unusual bottle types tend to contain wines at opposite ends of the quality spectrum: The most expensive Champagnes typically come in special bottles, with shapes that are unique to the brand. At the other end of the scale, some cheaply made wines attempt to disguise their lack of character with an attention-getting container.

This chapter introduces you to the key items you need to know about wine bottles. You learn how to decipher what the shape of the bottle means and also what to look for on the label.

The Basic Shapes

Wine bottles come in several predominant shapes, each with its own variations. You find these shapes most often:

➤ **Claret**   The Claret bottle, also called *Red Bordeaux*, has straight sides and sharp shoulders. This shape is used for wines made in the Bordeaux style, as well as wines grown and bottled on Bordeaux soil. Red Bordeaux, Sauternes, and Graves wines are all packaged in this angular bottle. So are Bordeaux-style California varietals, such as Cabernet Sauvignon, Merlot, Sauvignon Blanc, Semillon (all Bordeaux vinifera), and Zinfandel.

➤ **Burgundy**   Wines fuller in body or richer in perfume than Bordeaux-style wines are generally bottled in the narrow-shoulder, rounder Burgundy bottle. California Chardonnay and Pinot Noir— Burgundy varietals—are sold in the Burgundy bottle. Fuller-bodied Spanish wines and the sturdier Italian wines (such as Barolo and Barbaresco) find their way into variants of this shape.

➤ **Hock**   The German Hock bottle is tall, slender, and brown. Its variant is the green bottle traditionally used for Mosel wines. The traditional rule in Germany is Rhine wine in brown bottles, Mosel in green. This rule is no longer 100 percent true, but it still serves as a good guide. Most wines from Alsace are bottled in a shape similar to the Hock. So are many California Rieslings, Gewürztraminers, and Sylvaner varietals. The Hock shape is used throughout the world, but be warned: It is not always an indicator of the kind or quality of wine within.

Wine Wisdom

If you're the proud owner of a brand-new pleasure vessel that you'd like to christen with a magnum of bubbly, Champagne companies make special christening bottles for that purpose. You'd need an awful lot of muscle to smash the solid, reinforced glass of a real Champagne bottle.

➤ **Champagne** The bubbly bottle is sort of a bigger and sturdier cousin of the Burgundy bottle. It usually has an indentation or *punt* at the bottom, and extra-thick walls to withstand the pressure of the carbonation. As mentioned at the beginning of the chapter, the most expensive Champagnes are usually bottled in signature shapes. Also note the flaring Champagne cork: a laminated, seven-piece closure constructed to guarantee a tight, strong seal once it is in the bottle neck.

The reason for the deep green or brown color of most wine bottles is more than aesthetics: The color protects the wine from sunlight. (You wear sunglasses—why shouldn't your wine?) Brown glass is believed to offer even more protection than green, and it is often used for low-alcohol, sweet-finished white wines. All in all, though, technology is supplanting tradition. With advances in winemaking and better methods of stabilizing wines for bottle aging, clear glass is becoming more popular. Even traditional winemakers are giving in to the adage, "What you see is what you get."

The varied shapes of wine bottles.

Magnums and More

In addition to different shapes, wine bottles come in varying sizes. The standard size is 750 ml, which is approximately four-fifths of a quart. The other most common sizes are the half-bottle, which holds 375 ml, and the magnum, which holds 1.5 liters, or two standard bottles' worth of wine. A double magnum holds three liters, or four standard bottles. A Jeroboam holds six standard wine bottles, and an Impériale holds eight.

In Champagne, France, bottle sizes are somewhat different. A magnum is still a magnum, but a Jeroboam holds four standard bottles, not six; rather, the Rehoboam contains six standard bottles. A Methuselah contains eight standard bottles; a Salmanazar contains 12 standard bottles; a Balthazar contains 16 standard bottles; and a Nebuchadnezzar contains 20 standard bottles, perfect for large weddings or other momentous occasions.

The Vintage Makes It Right

The date on the bottle is the wine's vintage. It tells you the year the grapes were harvested and nothing more. The fact that there is a date on a bottle is not an indication of quality by itself, although most wines with a vintage do happen to be quality wines. That said, some everyday wines for which the vintage is of no importance will carry a vintage date just to make them appear better than they are. To determine whether the vintage was a good, great, or poor one for the region in question, you need to consult a vintage chart. Check the one on the tearout card in the front of this book, or look in wine magazines and newsletters for the lowdown on the latest vintages.

In a good vintage, certain weather conditions were met the entire year: Mother Nature smiled on the tender succulents, allowing the grapes to bathe, nap, and gradually reawaken refreshed and energetic, with just the right balance of acid, sugar, and flavors.

In a great vintage year, the quality of wine is unbelievable. Every flavor nuance is ready and waiting to incite your nose and taste buds into a peak sensory mode. The balance is perfect, the breed has been bred, and the wine has a body and concentration that other wines only dream of. How do you know which vintages have been so favored? Simply consult a vintage chart. Investing in a fine wine should not be a matter of trial and error; sometimes it's a good idea just to let someone else do the work.

Avoid poor vintages; the wines will be feeble, insipid, and vapid—not exactly what you want to start your wine collection. You should know, however, that even poor vintages have some properties that make for a good wine. You can find out which wines are good ones by reading reviews in wine magazines, in newsletters, or through online sources. Wine drinkers tend to malign average vintages, but doing so is really unfair. True, average vintages lack the complexity and finesse of a great vintage, but they're quite capable of providing a savvy consumer with some perfectly delightful wines—usually at reasonable prices.

Back Label Secrets

The back label *doesn't* have a picturesque scene of the vineyard, or a name like Château d'Yquem heralded by its royal crown. If one exists, the back label frequently contains interesting, if not useful, information. This is where bottlers might tell you which foods are a good match for the wine or what temperature brings out its peak flavor. The label may also offer an engaging story about the wine or the winery. Or it may tell you nothing more than the pH balance, if that. Front labels are regulated; back labels are a little more whimsical.

Bottling Terms

If you've been studying up on your AOC, QmP, DOCG, and AVA, you're probably starting to think that a wine label resembles a legal document or a Web site. Terms like these appear on the label, most by legal designation, to let you know what is in the bottle you're contemplating taking home.

All labels on wines sold in the United States must be approved by the Bureau of Alcohol, Tobacco and Firearms (BATF), a division of the Treasury Department. In addition to collecting alcohol taxes, BATF is charged with ensuring that the information on a wine bottle is truthful, straightforward, and accurate. All wines must conform both to the mandatory U.S. label requirements and to the regulations of the country of origin. Each state may also impose its own individual regulations, but these must conform to federal standards.

The philosophy in the United States seems to be *"Keep it simple."* This practice has its good and bad points. On the negative side is the fact that the domestic wine label is by far the least useful guide for determining the contents of the bottle (although many producers do choose to provide precise technical information). On the plus side, the more concise the terms on the label, the less likely they are to mislead buyers. Wine labels from all of the EU (European Union) countries must meet strict standards, which make them relatively easy to decipher. You simply need to know what to look for:

➤ **Origin Descriptors**   An *origin descriptor* refers to the words on the label that indicate where the wine comes from. The descriptor starts with a designation such as *Product of France* or *Product of Spain*, which is legally required of all imported wines. The descriptor goes on down through region, state, vineyard, château—whatever level of description is required for the particular type or quality of the wine.

➤ **Quality Descriptors**   By EU regulations, the wine with the vineyard name on the label is inherently of better quality than the wine that lists only a vast region. As you remember from earlier chapters, AOC, DOC, DOCG, and QmP are all quality indicators at the most basic level. Each country then has its own list of terms to describe the quality of the wine in the bottle (which we will get to soon in this chapter).

Grape Alert

European labels always designate the classification of the wine according to EU, national, and local regulations. American labels lack this quality indicator, and instead provide a lot of data concerning who grew the grapes and who selected, produced, or cellared the wine. If all you want is to choose the right wine, you might feel like you're reading a weather report for every city but your own.

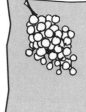

Grape Alert

Some domestic wine labels carry the quality descriptor *Classic*, but the term is virtually meaningless; these wines rarely *are* classic.

➤ **Style Descriptors**   Style descriptors are legally required only on German wines and Champagne. These descriptors indicate the wine's sweetness or dryness (percentage of residual sugar). Some non-German wine labels do include style descriptors, but whether or not this designator is included is at the discretion of the individual producer. The absence of a style descriptor is just one more reason to know your wines.

➤ **General Terms**   The most basic general terms are *white*, *red*, and *rosé* in the language of the wine's native land. Other general terms include virtually anything that doesn't fall into any of the previous categories. You might see the term *Table Wine* (required on imports; optional on domestic wines) or *Serve at room temperature* or *Serve chilled*. These tidbits of information, however, are entirely optional by the wine producer.

➤ **Mandatory Information**   Along with the country of origin, the alcoholic content and content by volume are absolutely imperative on all labels. Volume of imported wines is listed in standard metric measure and conforms to approved size. The name and address of the importer, producer, and/or négociant are required on all labels. For California wines, the name and address of the bottler and the Bonded Winery (BW) license number are required.

Only on American wines are varietal names mandatory.

The French Wine Label

The French wine label provides a lot of clues as to the ultimate quality of the wine. The label provides exacting information as to certain minimum quality standards through its system of Appellation Contrôlée regulations, which are linked to carefully defined geography. By law, the smaller the piece of property named, the more stringent the regulations are for methods of cultivation and production. Other than names of properties and estates, the names of the négociant (if any) and importer must appear on the label, so knowing the reputations of these companies is useful. Frequently, the name of the négociant or shipper is a clue to the quality of a wine from an unknown property.

A Bordeaux wine label.

A Burgundy wine label.

French Origin Descriptors

As you know by now, the letters *AOC* or *AC* on a label are an abbreviation of *Appellation d'Origine Contrôlée.* Here are some other terms you should know:

➤ *VDQS* stands for Vin Délimités de QualitéSupérieure, the second rank of delimited wine areas, below AC.

➤ *Vin de pays* is the third rank below AC.

➤ *Cave* is the French word for cellar.

➤ *Château-bottled, Mis au Château, Mis en bouteilles au Château, Mis au (or du) Domaine,* and *Mis en bouteilles au (or du) Domaine* all mean estate-bottled and have legal significance.

➤ *Mis dans nos caves, Mis par le Propriétaire,* and *Mis en bouteille à la Propriété* sound like estate-bottled wine but are not and are usually put on a label to deceive the consumer. These terms are not legally regulated.

➤ *Négociant* is a businessman who purchases wine from growers and bottles it under his own brand or for resale under the individual Château name.

➤ *Eleveur* is a négociant who buys young wine from the grower and matures it in his own cellars.

➤ *Propriétaire-Récolant* means owner and manager of a property.

French Quality Descriptors

Appellation Contrôlée is both an origin descriptor and a quality descriptor, as French geographical designations are linked to quality regulations. Other quality descriptors include the following:

➤ *Cru Classé* is a classified growth of Bordeaux, the most famous of which is the 1855 classification of the wines of the Médoc. It is preceded by the level of the cru such as *Premier Cru Classé*.

➤ *Cru Bourgeois* in Bordeaux refers to the many good vineyards just below the classified growths in quality.

➤ *Cru Exceptionnel* is a Bordeaux classification between Cru Bourgeois and Cru Classé.

➤ *Grand Cru* means "great growth"—in Burgundy the highest level of classified vineyards, in Bordeaux the highest of the five levels of classified growths.

➤ *Premier Cru* means "first growth"—in Burgundy the second level of classified growth, in Bordeaux any of the five levels of classified growths.

➤ *Grand Vin* means "great wine." As it has no legal definition, this term is used with impunity for any wine, good or otherwise.

➤ *Méthode Champenoise* (meaning *"fermented in this bottle"*) is the legally defined term for the Champagne method of sparkling wine production.

➤ *Supérieure* indicates that the wine is at least one degree of alcohol above the minimum allowed for a particular AC. The term does not mean that the wine is *better* or *superior*.

➤ *VDQS* and *Vin de pays* relate to the quality of a non-AC wine.

French Style Descriptors

Vin Blanc means white wine, *Vin Rouge* means red wine, and *Vin Rosé* means rosé wine. *Sur lie* refers to wines bottled off the lees without racking or filtering. *Pétillant* means slightly sparkling or crackling. *Mousseux* refers to sparkling wine other than Champagne. *Blanc de Blancs* refers to a white wine made entirely from white grapes; you usually see the term on Champagne bottles. With Champagne and Mousseux, *Brut* means almost dry; *Extra Dry* means slightly sweeter than Brut; *Brut Sauvage* or *Sauvage* means completely dry; *Demi-Sec* means semisweet; and *Doux* means quite sweet.

French General Terms

Année means year. *Recolte* means crop or harvest, and *Vendange* means grape harvest, used synonymously with année. *Chai* is an above-ground building where wine is stored in cask. *Chambré* is the French word for bringing a red wine from cellar temperature to room temperature (as in *Servir Chambre*, or *serve at room temperature*). *Servir Frais* means serve chilled. *Château in Bordeaux* refers to a single estate—elsewhere it may be part of a brand name. *Domaine* means wine estate. *Clos* means walled vineyard. *Côte* refers to a slope with vineyards as opposed to graves or flatter land. *Cru* means growth and refers to a legally defined vineyard. *Cuvée* is a vat or batch of wine.

The German Wine Label

The German wine label is exceedingly precise about quality; the descriptions are linked closely to growing regions—whether large and tiny, to a designation of quality, and also to the degree of ripeness achieved by the grapes that went into the wine. The labels often appear more complicated than they are, but they are less intimidating once you learn the system. The region in which the wine is produced and the ripeness of the grapes are the two main concerns, and both items play important roles on the label.

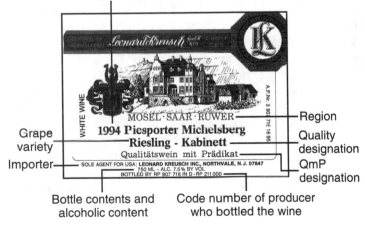

Vintage year and wine name (note Grosslage name looks just like a vineyard name but isn't)

Grape variety

Importer

Region

Quality designation

QmP designation

Bottle contents and alcoholic content

Code number of producer who bottled the wine

The German Grosslage wine label.

Vintage year and wine name (this
is an authentic vineyard name)

The German Einzellage wine label.

German Origin Descriptors

Gebiet is a term indicating one of the 13 major German
wine regions. A *Bereich* is a large subregion of a Gebiet. A
Grosslage is a subdivision of a Bereich consisting of numerous adjoining vineyards that may span the boundaries of
many villages. Grosslage wines are designated with a
name that sounds like an individual vineyard wine; therefore, you need to memorize Grosslage names to avoid
buying a village wine when you want a higher-quality
wine (see Appendix A). An *Einzellage* is an individual vineyard site of a minimum size of approximately 12 acres.
Vineyards smaller than 12 acres are given the name of a
nearby Einzellage and are of similar quality and style.

Here's a list of German terms to help you decipher the
wine labels:

➤ *Abfüller* means bottler, and *Abfüllung* means from
the producer's own estate.

➤ *Aus Eigenem Lesegut* and *Erzeuger Abfüllung* mean
estate-bottled.

➤ *Eigene Abfullung* means bottled by the producer.

➤ *Keller* is a cellar and *Weinkellerei* is a wine cellar.

➤ *Weingut* means wine estate, and *Weinhandler* refers to a wine shipper or merchant.

➤ *Winzergenossenschaft* and *Winzerverein* mean winegrower's cooperative.

➤ *Amtliche Prufungsunummer* (A.P.) is the official testing number found on all better German wines; it indicates the place of origin, the producer's individual number, the individual lot number, and the year (not necessarily the vintage) that the lot was submitted for testing.

German Quality Descriptors

Tafelwein is table wine, the lowest level of quality. Tafelwein may not bear a vineyard site name. *Qualitätswein bestimmter Anbaugebiete* (QbA) refers to a wine from a specific origin and is the middle level of German wine quality. *Qualitätswein mit Prädikat* (QmP) refers to wine with special attributes, the top level of wine quality consisting of six degrees of ripeness. No chaptalization is permitted for these wines.

German Style Descriptors

Kabinett is the basic grade for QmP wine that's made from grapes with enough natural sugar to produce a wine with a minimum of 9.5 percent alcohol. *Spätlese* means late picked and refers to a wine made from fully ripened grapes. *Auslese* is a term describing very ripe, late-picked grapes that render a fairly sweet and luscious dessert wine. *Beerenauslese* is a very sweet wine made from even later-picked, overripe grapes, some of which have been shriveled by Botrytis (noble rot). *Tröckenbeerenauslese* is wine made entirely from grapes shriveled by Botrytis. During the harvest, the pickers keep these grapes separate from the others. *Eiswein* is a sweet, concentrated wine made from frozen grapes that may not be affected with Botrytis. *Tröcken* refers to a complete dry wine. *Halbtröcken* is a half-dry or off-dry wine. *Perlwein* is a slightly sparkling wine, and *Sekt* means "sparkling wine."

German General Terms

Moselblumchen is the generic wine from the Mosel that is in the Tafelwein class. *Liebfraumilch* is the generic wine from the Rhein region that is in the QbA class. *Fass* and *fuder* mean cask. *Rotwein* means red wine, and *Weisswein* means white wine. *Schloss* means castle. *Staatswein* refers to wine from government-owned vineyards.

The Italian Wine Label

Italian wine labels provide a fair amount of meaningful information. Nomenclature for certain wines is regulated under laws enacted in 1967, modeled after the French concept but without the refinement of official classifications. The Italian wine-regulating system, the *Denominazione di Origine Controllata* (DOC) is government approved and defines growing regions. For several types of wine, the DOC guarantees certain minimum standards of production. Good-quality Italian wines indicate the place, either as the name of the wine itself (Chianti, for example), linked to a grape variety (such as Barbera D'Asti), or through a DOC designation. Not all places have earned DOC status, but most better Italian wines sold within the United States are DOC wines. If a grape name is not referenced by a place, (such as Nebbiolo d'Alba), chances are that the wine lacks distinction. *Denominazione di Origine Controllata e Garantita* (DOCG) is the highest grade of Italian wine and is granted only to regions making the highest-quality wine.

Wine name
Wine district
Producer

NOZZOLE

CHIANTI CLASSICO
DENOMINAZIONE DI ORIGINE CONTROLLATA E GARANTITA

RISERVA 1993

ESTATE BOTTLED BY
TENIMENTI AGRICOLI VALDIGREVE S.A.S.
GREVE - ITALIA

RED WINE
PRODUCT OF ITALY

750 ML
13% ALC BY VOL.

DOCG quality designation
Estate-bottled designation

Riserva quality designation with vintage date
Alcoholic content
Bottle contents

The Italian wine label.

Italian Origin Descriptors

DOC refers to a wine from a delimited wine district, produced in accordance with DOC wine laws. *DOCG* is wine made from a delimited district that has earned this higher-quality designation. Following are some other helpful origin descriptors:

➤ *Classico* refers to a wine made in a legally defined inner section of a wine district and ostensibly denotes a higher quality.

➤ *Cantina* means winery or cellars, and *Cantina Sociale* is a winegrower's cooperative.

➤ *Casa Vinicola* means wine company.

➤ *Consorzio* is a local winegrower's association with legal recognition.

➤ *Infiascato alla fattoria, Imbottigliato nell'origine, Imbottigliato del produttore,* and *Messo in bottiglia nell'origine* mean estate bottled.

➤ *Imbottigliato nello stabilimento della ditta* means bottled on the premises of the company; this wine is not estate-bottled.

➤ *Tenuta* refers to a farm or agricultural holding.

Italian Quality Descriptors

DOC and *DOCG*, explained earlier, are quality descriptors. *Riserva* means aged in wood for a time specified by law. *Riserva Speciale* indicates that the wine was aged one year longer than Riserva. *Stravecchio* means very old; this term is rarely seen.

Italian Style Descriptors

Secco means dry. *Amaro* means very dry (bitter). *Abboccato* and *amabile* mean off-dry or semisweet with amabile being sweeter than abboccato. *Dolce* means sweet. *Cotto* refers to a concentrated wine. *Passito* refers to wine made from semidried grapes. *Spumante* is sparkling wine, and *Frizzante* is semisparkling wine. *Vin santo* is wine made from grapes dried indoors.

Italian General Terms

Vino da Tavola means table wine. *Bianco* means white wine; *rosso* means red wine; and *rosato* means rosé wine. *Nero* is very dark red. *Fiasco* is a flask.

The American Wine Label

In terms of legally defined nomenclature, very little on an American wine label is useful in differentiating a high-quality wine from an ordinary wine. Terms such as *Reserve*, *Special Reserve*, *Vintner's Reserve*, and so on, have no legal regulation and may be used with impunity on mediocre or low-quality wines. Also, American wine districts are required only to defining geography, and unlike the French, Italians, and Germans, do not have any concomitant regulations determining grape variety, yield, or production methods.

To tell the difference between two wines from a particular wine district (Napa Valley, for example), you must have an intimate knowledge of the individual producers. Although some districts are reputed to be better than others, a well-made wine from a lesser district can be far superior to a wine made from large yields in a more respected district. With American wine, *caveat emptor* is the rule, and the U.S. government has no interest in establishing regulations that can give you clues as to which wine is better than another.

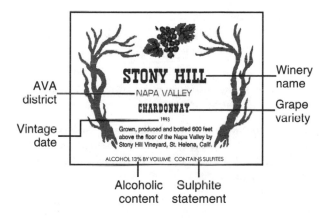

The American wine label.

American Origin Descriptors

American indicates that the wine can be a blend of wines from different states. *State* indicates that 75 percent of the wine must be from the named state; California regulations, however, require that California wine be 100 percent Californian. *County* indicates that 75 percent of the wine must be from the named county. *Valley*, *District*, and *Region* must be a BATF-approved *American Viticultural Area* (AVA) to be used on the label, and at least 75 percent of the wine must come from the named area. The general rule of thumb is that the smaller the geographical area specified, the better the reputed quality, but there's no guarantee. The following list of descriptors will help you further decipher American wine labels:

➤ *B.W. No.* is the bonded winery's license number.

➤ *Grown by* indicates that the grapes were grown by the named winery.

➤ *Selected by* indicates that the wine was purchased by the named winery.

➤ *Made and Bottled by* indicates that the named winery fermented at least 10 percent of the wine and bottled all the wine.

➤ *Cellared and Bottled by* indicates that the named party blended and/or aged or otherwise treated and bottled all the wine.

➤ *Produced and Bottled by, Proprietor or Vintner Grown,* and *Bottled by* indicates that the named party fermented at least 75 percent of the wine and bottled all the wine.

➤ *Estate Bottled* means that the named party fermented all the wine from grapes 100 percent from the named AVA; that the grapes came entirely from the party's own vineyards or vineyards in which the party controls the viticultural practices; and that the wine was bottled on the same premises where it was made.

American Quality Descriptors

Reserve, *Vintner's Reserve*, and *Special Reserve* are label puffery that have no legal definition. In some cases, these terms designate the best of the producer's wine, and in other cases, the wine is no different or is actually lesser in quality than the producer's regular line of wine. *Rare* or

Classic, usually seen on the most inexpensive wine, has no legal definition—the wine so labeled is rarely "rare" or "classic." Here are some terms that *do* mean something:

➤ *Nouveau* refers to wines that were quickly fermented by carbonic maceration and bottled immediately after fermentation.

➤ *Late Harvest* refers to wine made from overripe grapes, which may or may not have been affected with Botrytis.

➤ *Brix* is a measure of potential alcohol based on the sugar content of the grape when it was harvested.

➤ *Residual sugar* refers to the amount of remaining natural sugar in the wine after fermentation is completed—more than one percent residual sugar tastes sweet.

➤ *Off-dry* refers to wine that has a little residual sugar but not enough to be sweet.

➤ *Botrytis* means the grapes were affected with Botrytis.

➤ *Fermented in the bottle* refers to sparkling wine made by the "transfer method." *Fermented in this bottle* refers to sparkling wine made by *Méthode Champenoise,* which makes for better bubbles and taste.

American General Terms

Table wine refers to wine that is less than 14.5 percent alcohol and made without additional alcohol. *Dessert wine* is more than 14.5 percent alcohol and is usually sweet wine fortified with additional alcohol. *White* is white wine; *red* is red wine; and *rosé* or *blush* is rosé wine.

Recommended Wines

The following lists are my recommendations of the nationally distributed wines that represent consistent quality and good value. The wine region follows the wine name in parentheses. Prices are for regular 750ml bottles unless otherwise indicated. Prices are full-markup retail prices—you should find these wines at lower prices at discount stores.

Recommended Red Wines Under $8

Belle Jour (France) $7.99 (1.5L)

Bodegas Montecello (Rioja, Spain) $6.50

Casal Thaulero Montepulciano D'Abruzzo (Italy) $7.99 (1.5L)

Castello di Gabbiano Chianti Classico (Italy) $7.99

Château Gourgazaud (Minervois, France) $7.50

Château Pitray 1994 (Bordeaux, France) $7.99

Concha y Toro Cabernet Sauvignon/Merlot (Chile) $7.99 (1.5L)

Dessilani Spanna (Piedmont, Italy) $7.99

Fetzer Valley Oaks Cabernet Sauvignon (California) $7.50

La Vieille Ferme (Côtes Ventoux, France) $7.50

Los Vascos Cabernet Sauvignon (Chile) $6.99

Monte Antico (Tuscany, Italy) $7.99

Napa Ridge Winery Cabernet Sauvignon (California) $7.99

Rosemont Estate Shiraz/ Cabernet Sauvignon (Australia) $6.99

Serradayres (Portugal) $5.99

Vendange Cabernet Sauvignon (California) $7.99 (1.5L)

Recommended White Wines Under $8

Alianca Vinho Verde (Portugal) $4.99

Boucheron Blanc de Blanc (France) $6.99 (1.5L)

Hogue Fumé Blanc (Washington State) $7.99

Joseph Brigl Pinot Grigio (Italy) $6.99

Casa Lapostolle Sauvignon Blanc (Chile) $6.50

Château Bonnet Blanc (Bordeaux, France) $6.99

Château du Cleray Muscadet (France) $7.99

Concha y Toro Sauvignon/ Semillon (Chile) $6.99 (1.5L)

Domaine de Pouy (France) $5.99

Fetzer Sundial Chardonnay (California) $6.99

La Vieille Ferme Blanc (France) $6.99

Louis Latour Chardonnay (Ardeche, France) $6.99

Moreau Blanc (France) $7.49 (1.5L)

Rosemont Estate Semillon/ Chardonnay (Australia) $7

Vendange Chardonnay (California) $7.99 (1.5L)

Recommended Red Wines $8–$15

Beringer Knight's Valley Cabernet Sauvignon 1992 (California) $14.99

Ceretto Dolcetto D'Alba 1994 (Piedmont, Italy) $13.99

Château Meyney 1993 (St. Estèphe, France) $14.99

Domaine Sorin 1994 (Côtes-de-Provence, France) $10.99

Filliatreau "Grand Vignolle" Saumur-Champigny 1995 (Loire, France) $13.99

Guigal Gigondas 1993 (France) $14.99

La Rioja Alta Vina Alberdi Reserva 1991 (Rioja, Spain) $12.99

Louis Latour Côte-de-Beaune-Villages 1993 (Burgundy, France) $12.99

Markham Merlot 1994 (California) $14.99

Melini Borghi D'Elsa Chianti (Italy) $10.99 (1.5L)

Mouton Cadet Rouge (Bordeaux, France) $14.99 (1.5L)

Penfold's Bin 389 Cabernet Sauvignon/Shiraz 1993 (Australia) $14.99

Robert Mondavi "Woodbridge" Cabernet Sauvignon (California) $12.99 (1.5L)

The Monterey Vineyard Classic Cabernet Sauvignon (California) 10.99 (1.5L)

Villa Antinori Chianti Classico Riserva 1993 (Italy) $13.99

Recommended White Wines $8-$15

Beringer Chardonnay Napa Valley 1994 (California) $11.99

Château Cruzeau Blanc 1994 (Bordeaux/Graves, France) $10.99

Chartran-Trebuchet Rully "La Chaume" 1995 (France) $14.99

Domaine Aubuisiers Vouvray Sec "Le Marigny" 1995 (France) $11.99

Fernand Girard Sancerre "La Garenne" 1995 (France) $12.99

Livio Felluga Pinot Grigio 1995 (Italy) $12.99

Paul Pernot Bourgogne Blanc 1994 (Burgundy France) $13.99

Rosemont Chardonnay "Show Reserve" 1994 (Australia) $13.99

Trimbach Riesling 1993 (Alsace, France) $13.99

Von Simmern Eltviller Sonnenberg Kabinett (Germany) $13.99

France—Recommended Red Wine Producers (Châteaux) of Bordeaux

In the following section, the Château name is followed by the district in parentheses.

Ausone (St.-Emilion)

Batailley (Pauillac)

Beauséjour-Duffau (St.-Emilion)

Bon Pasteur (Pomerol)

Branaire-Ducru (St.-Julien)

Calon-Ségur (St.-Estèphe)

Canon (St.-Emilion)

Canon-La-Gaffelière (St.-Emilion)

Certan de May (Pomerol)

Chasse-Spleen (Moulis)

Margaux (Margaux)

Clerc Milon (Pauillac)

Clinet (Pomerol)

Cos d'Estournel (St.-Estèphe)

Cos Labory (St.-Estèphe)

Daugay (St.-Emilion)

de Fieuzal (Graves)

Domaine de Chevalier (Graves)

Ducru-Beaucaillou (St.-Julien)

Duhart-Milon-Rothschild (Pauillac)

d'Angludet (Margaux)

Ferrand-Lartique (St.-Emilion)

Figeac (St.-Emilion)

Forcas-Hosten (Listrac)

Gazin (Pomerol)

Giscours (Margaux)

Gloria (St.-Julien)

Grand-Mayne (St.-Emilion)

Grand-Puy-Ducasse (Pauillac)

Grand-Puy-Lacoste (Pauillac)

Gruad-Larose (St.-Julien)

Haut-Bages-Libéral (Pauillac)

Haut-Bailly (Graves)

Haut-Batailley (Pauillac)

Haut-Brion (Graves)

Haut-Marbuzet (St.-Estèphe)

La Conseillante (Pomerol)

La Fleur de Gay (Pomerol)

La Mission-Haut-Brion (Graves)

La Dominique (St.-Emilion)

La Fleur Pétrus (Pomerol)

La Lagune (Ludon)

La Louvière (Graves)

Lafite-Rothschild (Pauillac)

Lafleur (Pomerol)

Lafon-Rochet (St.-Estèphe)

Lagrange (St.-Julien)

Langoa-Barton (St.-Julien)

Latour (Pauillac)

Latour à Pomerol (Pomerol)

Le Pin (Pomerol)

Le Tertre-Roteboeuf (St.-Emilion)

Les-Ormes-de-Pez (St.-Estèphe)

Léoville-Las-Cases (St.-Julien)

Léoville-Barton (St.-Julien)

Léoville-Poyferré (St.-Julien)

Lynch-Bages (Pauillac)

L'Angélus (St.-Emilion)

L'Arrosée (St.-Emilion)

L'Eglise-Clinet (Pomerol)

L'Evangile (Pomerol)

Montose (St.-Estèphe)

Moulin-Pey-Labrie (Canon-Fronsac)

Mouton-Rothschild (Pauillac)

Palmer (Margeaux)

Pape-Clément (Graves)

Pavie-Macquin (St.-Emilion)

Petit-Village (Pomerol)

Pétrus (Pomerol)

Phélan-Ségur (St.-Estèphe)

Pichon-Longueville Baron (Pauillac)

Pichon-Longueville-Comtesse de Laland (Pauillac)

Pontet-Canet (Pauillac)

Prieuré-Lichine (Margaux)

Rausan-Séglas (Margaux)

Smith-Haut-Lafitte (Graves)

Talbot (St.-Julien)

Troplong-Mondot (St.-Emilion)

Trotanoy (Pomerol)

Valandraud (St.-Emilion)

Vieux Château Certan (Pomerol)

France—Recommended White Wine Producers (Châteaux) of Bordeaux

In the following section, the Château name is followed by the district in parentheses.

Bouscaut (Graves)

Carbonnieux (Graves)

de Malle (Graves)

Clos Floridène (Graves)

Couhins-Lurton (Graves)

de Fieuzal (Graves)

Doisy-Daëne (Bordeaux)

Domaine de Chevalier (Graves)

Haut-Brion Blanc (Graves)

La Louvière (Graves)

La Tour-Martillac (Graves)

Laville-Haut-Brion (Graves)

Loudenne (Bordeaux)

Pape-Clément (Graves)

Pavillon Blanc de Château Margaux (Bordeaux)

R de Rieussec (Graves)

Respide (Graves)

Smith-Haut-Lafitte (Graves)

France—Recommended Wine Producers (Châteaux) of Bordeaux, Sauternes/Barsac

In the following section, the Château name is followed by the district in parentheses.

Climens (Barsac)

Caillou (Barsac)

Clos Haut-Peyraguey (Sauternes)

Coutet (Barsac)

Doisy-Daëne (Barsac)

Doisy-Dubroca (Barsac)

de Fargues (Sauternes)

Filhot (Sauternes)

Gilette (Sauternes)

Guiraud (Sauternes)

La Tour Blanche (Sauternes)

Lafaurie-Peyraguey (Sauternes)

Rabaud-Promis (Sauternes)

Raymond-Lafon (Sauternes)

Rayne-Vigneau (Sauternes)

Rieussec (Sauternes)

Sigalas Rabaud (Sauternes)

Suduiraut (Sauternes)

France—Recommended Red Wine Producers of Burgundy

Armand Rousseau	Jacques Prieur
Barthod-Noellat	Jean Chauvenet
Bernard Dugat	Jean Grivot
Bertrand Ambroise	Jean Gros
Bouchard Père et Fils	Jean et J. L. Trapet
Bouré Père et Fils	Joseph Drouhin
Bourée-Noellat	Labourée-Roi
Chanson Père et Fils	Leroy
Claude et Maurice Dugat	Louis Latour
Comte Lafon	Louis Jadot
Comte de Vougüé	Marquis d'Angerville
Daniel Chopin-Groffier	Michel Lafarge
Daniel Rion	Michel Prunier
de l'Arlot	Mongeard-Mugneret
Domaine de la Romané-Conti	Philippe Leclerc
Dujac	Pierre Gelin
Faiveley	Ponsot
George et Chistophe Roumier	Ramonet
Haegelen-Jayer	Remoissenet Père et Fils
Henri Jayer	René Engel
Hospices de Beaune	René Leclerc
Hubert Lignier	Robert Arnoux
J.F. Coche-Dury	Robert Jayer-Gilles

France—Recommended White Wine Producers of Burgundy

Albert Grivault

Antonin Rodet

Ballot-Millot et Fils

Bernard Morey

Bouchard Père et Fils

Château de Meursault

Château de Puligny-Montrachet

Colin-Déléger

Comte Lafon

Domaine de la Romanée-Conti

Domaine de l'Arlot

Domaine Leflaive

Etienne Sauzet

Faiveley

Francois et Jean-Marie Raveneau

Georges Déléger

J.F. Coche-Dury

J. Moreau et Fils

Jacques Prieur

Jean-Philippe Fichet

Jean Dauvissat

Jean-Marc Boillot

Joseph Drouhin

Leroy

Louis Jadot

Louis Latour

Marc Colin

Marc Morey

Michel Niellon

Michelot-Buisson

Patrick Javillier

Philippe Testut

Pierre Boillot

Ramonet

Remoissenet Pere et Fils

René et Vincent Dauvissat

Thierry Matrot

Verget

Italy—Recommended Wine Producers of Piedmont

Aldo Conterno

Aldo & Ricardo Seghesio

Alfiero Boffa

Alfredo Prunotto

Angelo Gaja

Antoniolo

Azelia

Bartolomeo

Batasiolo

Bersano

Bruno Giacosa

Bruno Ceretto

Ceretto

Cerutti

Cigliuti

Clerico

Enrico Scavino

Fontanafredda

Francesco Rinaldi

G.D. Vajra

Giacomo Conterno

Guiseppe Mascarello

Luciano Sandrone

Manzone

Marcarini

Marchese di Gresy

Moccagatta

Paolo Conterno

Pio Cesare

Poderi Rocche Manzoni Valentino

Produttori di Barbaresco

Renato Corino

Renato Ratti

Roberto Voerzio

Vietti

Italy—Recommended Wine Producers of Tuscany

Altesino

Ambra

Azienda Agricola La Torre

Badia a Coltibuono

Barbi

Biondi-Santi

Caparzo

Case Basse

Castello dei Rampolla Sammarco

Castello di Ama

Castello di Gabbiano

Castello di Querceto

Castell'In Villa

Ciacci Piccolomini d'Aragona

Costanti

Dei

Felsina Berardenga

Fontodi

Frescobaldi

Il Poggione

Isole e Olena Collezione de Marchi l'Ermo

L. Antinori

Lisini

Melini

Monsanto

Monte Vertine

Nozzole

Ornellaia

P. Antinori

Pertimali

Podere Il Palazzino

Poggio Antico

Ruffino

San Felice

San Giusto a Rententano

Soldera

Villa Banfi

Villa Cafaggio

Germany—Recommended Wine Producers

Alfred Merkelbach (Mosel)

August Eser (Rheingau)

Christian Karp-Schreiber (Mosel)

Dr. Burklin-Wolf (Pfalz)

Dr. Loosen-St.-Johannishof (Mosel)

Dr. Thanisch (Mosel)

E. Jakoby-Mathy (Mosel)

Egon Müller (Saar)

F.W. Gymnasium (Mosel)

Freiherr von Heddesdorf (Mosel)

Freiherr zu Knyphausen (Rheingau)

Fritz Haag (Mosel)

H & R Lingenfelder (Rheinpfalz)

Heribert Kerpen (Mosel)

Immich-Batterieberg (Mosel)

J.F. Kimich (Rheinpfalz)

J.J. Christoffel (Mosel)

J.J. Prüm (Mosel)

Josef Deinhart (Mosel)

Klaus Neckerauer (Rheinpfalz)

Koehler-Ruprecht (Rheingau)

Konigin Victoria Berg-Deinhard (Rheingau)

Kurt Darting (Rheinpfalz)

Mönchhof (Mosel)

Schloss Schönborn (Rheingau)

Selbach-Oster (Mosel)

von Brentano (Rheingau)

von Kesselstatt (Mosel)

von Simmern (Rheingau)

Weingut Karlsmuhle (Mosel)

Willi Schaefer (Mosel)

Spain—Recommended Table Wine Producers

CVNE

Marqués de Murrieta

Pesquera

Vega Sicilia

René Barbier

Domecq

Marqués de Grinon

Jean Léon

Bodegas Muga

La Rioja Alta

Marqués de Riscal

Marqués de Caceres

Montecillo

Rioja Santiago

Miguel Torres

Frederico Paternina

Spain—Recommended Sherry Producers

Emilio Lustau

Gonzalez Byass

Osborne

Pedro Domecq

Sandeman

Vinicola Hidalgo

Portugal—Recommended Porto Producers

Churchill

Cockburn

Croft

Delaforce

Dow

Ferreria

Fonseca

Graham's

Niepoort

Offley

Quinta do Noval

Ramos-Pinto

Sandeman

Smith-Woodhouse

Taylor Fladgate

Warre

Portugal—Recommended Table Wine Producers

Carvalho, Ribeiro, Ferreira

Casal de Valle Pradinhos

Caves do Barrocas

Caves Dom Teodosio

Caves San João

Caves Velhas

Condo do Santar

Ferreira

J.M. Da Fonseca

João Pires

Luis Pato

Porta dos Cavalheiros

Quinta do Carmo

Quinta do Cotto

Quinta da Cismeira

Quinta do Confradeiro

Quinta da Lagoalva de Cima

Quinta de la Rosa

Sogrape

Tuella

Vasconcellos

Australia—Recommended Wine Producers

Berry Estates	Rosemount
Browen Estate	Rothbury Estate
Brown Brothers	Seppelt
Château Tahbilk	St. Hurbert
Hungerford	Taltarni
Lindemans	Tyrells
Mildara	Wolf Blass
Orlando	Wyndham Estates
Penfolds	Wynns
Peter Lehmann	Yarra Yering

California, Oregon, and Washington State— Recommended Cabernet Sauvignon Producers

Arrowood	Dry Creek
Beaulieu	Duckhorn
Benziger	Far Neinte
Beringer	Farrari-Carano
Burgess	Fetzer
Cain Cellars	Flora Springs
Cakebread	Franciscan
Caymus	Gallo—Sonoma
Château Montelena	Geyser Peak
Château St. Jean	Grace Family Vineyard
Château Souverain	Heitz
Château Potelle	Hess Collection
Clos du Val	Jospeh Phelps
Cuvaison	Justin
Dalla Valle	Kendall-Jackson
Dehlinger	Kenwood

Mount Veeder	Silverado
Newton	Simi
Opus One	Spring Mountain
Ridge	Stag's Leap Wine Cellars
Robert Mondavi	Stag's Leap Vintners
Robert Pecota	Sterling
S. Anderson	Vichon
Shafer	ZD

California, Oregon, and Washington State— Recommended Merlot Producers

Arrowood	Gary Farrel
Benziger	Joseph Phelps
Beringer	Kenwood
Cain Cellars	Matanzas Creek
Château St. Jean	Robert Pecota
Château Souverain	Robert Mondavi
Cuvaison	Robert Keenan
Duckhorn	Sterling
Ferrari-Carano	Whitehall Lane
Frog's Leap	

California, Oregon, and Washington State— Recommended Pinot Noir Producers

Acacia	Carneros Creek
Adelsheim	Caymus
Au Bon Climat	Château Souverain
Beaulieu	Conn Valley
Benziger	David Bruce
Bouchaine	Dehlinger
Calera	Domaine Drouhin

Etude

Gary Farrell

Kendall-Jackson

Meridian

Robert Mondavi

Robert Sinskey

Robert Stemmler

Saintsbury

Sanford

Santa Cruz Mountain

Wild Horse

Williams-Selyem

ZD

California, Oregon, and Washington State— Recommended Zinfandel Producers

Benziger

Beringer

Caymus

Château Souverain

Château Montelena

Château Potelle

De Loach

Dry Creek

Ferrari-Carano

Fetzer

Franciscan

Frick

Gallo—Sonoma

Grgich Hills

Guenoc

Gundlach-Bundschu

Hop Kiln

Kenwood

Lytton Springs

Quivira

Rabbit Ridge

Ravenswood

Ridge

Robert Mondavi

Rosenblum

Seghesio Winery

Sutter Home

Topolos

Wild Horse

California, Oregon, and Washington State— Recommended Chardonnay Producers

Acacia

Arrowood

Au Bon Climat

Bargetto

Benziger

Beringer

Bouchaine

Burgess Cellars

Cakebread

Calera

Carmenet

Carneros Creek

Chalone

Chappellet

Château Montelena

Château St. Jean

Château Ste. Michelle

Château Souverain

Château Woltner

Clos du Bois

Cronin

Cuvaison

De Loach

Dehlinger

Ferrari-Carano

Flora Springs

Franciscan

Freemark Abby

Gabrielli

Gallo—Sonoma

Girard

Gloria Ferrer

Grgich Hills

Hanzell

Hess Collection

Iron Horse

J. Lohr

Joseph Phelps

Kendall-Jackson

Kenwood

Matanzas Creek

Meridian

Mirassou

Murphy-Goode

Napa Ridge

Newton

Pahlmeyer

Qupé

Rabbit Ridge

Robert Mondavi

Robert Sinskey

Rombauer

S. Anderson

Saintsbury

Sanford

Simi

Sonoma Cutrer

Sonoma-Loeb

Stag's Leap Wine Cellars

Vichon

Williams-Selyem

ZD

California, Oregon, and Washington State— Recommended Sauvignon Blanc Producers

Araujo Estate	Guenoc Winery
Benziger	Iron Horse
Beringer	Kendall-Jackson
Cain	Kenwood
Cakebread	Matanzas Creek
Caymus	Murphy-Goode
Chalk Hill	Napa Ridge
Château Potelle	Navarro
Château St. Jean	Preston
De Loach	Quivira
Dry Creek	Robert Mondavi
Duckhorn	Robert Pepi
Ferrari-Carano	Seghesio
Fetzer	Simi
Flora Springs	Spottswoode
Geyser Peak	Stag's Leap Wine Cellars
Grgich Hills	Vichon

California, Oregon, and Washington State— Recommended Sparkling Wine Producers

Codorniu	Maison Deutz
Culbertson	Mirassou
Domaine Chandon	Monticello
Domaine Carneros	Mumm Napa
Domaine Ste. Michelle	Piper Sonoma
Gloria Ferrer	Roderer Estate
Handley	S. Anderson
Iron Horse	Scharffenberger
Korbel	Schramsberg

The Best-Known Grosslage Wines of Germany

These wines are from the large Grosslage district, even though they have generic names that appear to be a single vineyard (Einzellage) name. These wines are mostly simple everyday wines and should be inexpensive. Don't confuse these names with single vineyard names.

Mosel-Saar-Ruwer

Bernkasteler Badstube

Bernkastler Kurfürstlay

Erdener Schwarzlay

Graacher Munzlay

Krover Nactarsch

Piesporter Michelsberg

Trierer Romerley

Wiltinger Scharzberg

Zeller Scharzer Katz

The Nahe

Kreuznacher Kronenberg

Neiderhausener Burweg

Rudesheimer Rosengarten

Rheingau

Hattenheimer-Deutelsberg

Hochheimer Daubhaus

Johannisberger Erntebrigner

Rauenthaler Steinmacher

Rudesheim Burgweg

Rheinhessen

Bingener Sankt-Rochuskapelle

Niersteiner Gutes Domtal

Niersteiner Rehbach

Niersteiner Spiegelberg

Oppenheimer-Krotenbrunnen

Oppenheimmer-Guldenmorgen

Rheinphalz (Palatinate)

Bockenheimer Gafenstuck

Deiderheimer Hofstuck

Durkheimer Hochmess

Foster Mariengarten

Wachenheimer Schenkenbohl

Appendix B

Glossary

The following glossary of terms goes beyond the list of terms included in the "Wine Word" sidebars throughout this book. Here, I've laid out a full glossary of wine lingo that will send you on your way to a full understanding and appreciation of wine (and it'll help you hold your own in any wine-snob's conversation, to boot).

acidic   A description of wine whose total acidity is so high that it imparts a sharp feel or sour taste in the mouth.

acidity   Refers to the nonvolatile acids in a wine, principally tartaric, malic, and citric. These acids provide a sense of freshness and balance to a wine. Excessive acidity provides a sharp or sour taste; too little results in a flat or flabby character.

aftertaste   The lingering impression of a wine after it is swallowed. It is usually described as the *"finish"* of a wine. It ranges from short to lingering. A lingering aftertaste is indicative of a quality wine.

aged   Describes a wine that has been cellared either in cask or in bottle long enough to have developed or improved. As a tasting term it describes the characteristic scent and taste of a wine that has so developed while in bottle.

astringent   A puckering, tactile sensation imparted to the wine by its tannins. A puckering quality adds to the total sense of the wine, giving it a sense of structure, style, and vitality. Tannins are an essential component in red wines, which are made to improve with age in the bottle. Red wines lacking in tannins are generally dull and uninteresting. Wines vinified for prolonged aging are harshly tannic when young, but mellow when the wine's age and the tannins precipitate to form a sediment in the bottle.

Auslese   Literally, "picked out" (i.e., selected). Under the new German wine law, Auslese wines are those that are subject to all regulations included in *Qualitätswein mit Prädikat* (quality wine with special attributes). Auslese wine is made entirely from selected, fully ripe grapes with all unripened and diseased grapes removed. No sugar may be added. The wine is especially full, rich, and somewhat sweet.

balance   Refers to the proportion of the various elements of a wine: acid against sweetness, fruit flavors against wood, and tannic alcohol against acid and flavor.

barrel fermented   Refers to the fermentation of a wine in a small oak cask as opposed to a large tank or vat.

Beerenauslese   "Berry-selected," or individual grape berries picked out (by order of ripeness) at harvest for their sugar content, quality, and amount of *Edelfaule* (noble rot).

Blanc de Blancs   Describes a white wine made from white grapes. The term refers to both still table and sparkling wines. The words Blanc de Blancs do not signify a quality better than other white wines.

Bodega   In the Spanish wine trade, a wine house, wine company, wine cellar, or even wine shop.

body   The tactile impression of fullness on the palate caused by the alcohol, glycerin, and residual sugar in a wine. The extremes of body are full and thin.

Botrytis Cinerea   A species of mold that attacks grapes grown in moist conditions. It is undesirable for most grape varieties or when it infects a vineyard prior to the grapes reaching full maturity. That said, when Botrytis attacks fully mature grapes and causes them to shrivel, both the acidity and the sugar in the grapes are concentrated, resulting in an intensified flavor and a desired sweetness balanced by acidity.

breed   A term used to describe the loveliest, most harmonious, and refined wines that achieve what is called "classical proportions." The term is elusive to definition, but wines that deserve such acclaim are unmistakable when encountered.

cooperage   Refers to the wooden barrels and tanks used for aging wines.

Cru Bourgeois   Refers to red Bordeaux wines from the Haut-Médoc that rank just below the Grande Cru Classé wines of the 1855 Bordeaux classification.

Cru Classé   Literally, "classified growth." Refers to those wines originally classified as Grand Cru Classé in the 1855 Bordeaux classification.

crush   Commonly used to refer to the grape harvest or vintage. Most specifically refers to the breaking of the grape stems, which begins the fermentation process.

cuve   A large vat, usually made of wood, used for the fermentation of grape juice into wine.

cuvée   Refers to the contents of a wine vat. More loosely used to refer to all the wine made at one time or under similar conditions. Sometimes refers to a specific pressing or batch of wine. Sometimes used as part of a brand name or trademark, or as wine label nomenclature to refer to a batch of wine.

dosage   A small amount of sugar, champagne, and brandy, which is added to Champagne right after degorgement. The final sweetness of the wine is determined by this step.

Eleveur   Refers to a wine firm that cares for wines in their barrels and bottles them, frequently blending to provide better structure and balance. Often, this firm is also a négociant or shipper.

estate bottled   Refers to a wine that has been bottled at the vineyard or winery where it was made. This term has legal significance in several countries, particularly France, Germany, and Italy, but it is not controlled in others. Basically, it connotes wine that was under the control of the winemaker from vineyard to bottle. Although many years ago the term assured the excellence of a wine, today it does not.

fermentation   The process of converting sugar into alcohol, usually by the action of yeast on the juice of fruit, such as grapes. It is a complex process in which the yeast produces enzymes that convert the sugar into alcohol, carbon dioxide, and heat.

finesse   A quality of elegance that separates a fine wine from simply a good wine. It is a harmony of flavors and components rarely found in wine. The term is hard to define, but like wine with breed, a wine with finesse is unmistakable when encountered.

fining   A clarifying technique that introduces an electrolytic agent, such as egg white, powered milk, blood, diatomaceous earth (bentonite), or gelatin, to attract the solids and settle them to the bottom of a cask. Beaten egg whites or bentonite are the most frequently used agents.

finish   The aftertaste of a wine when it has been swallowed. Usually consists of both flavor and tactile sensations from the acidity, alcohol, and tannins of the wine.

flor A film of yeast or bacteria, usually in cask on top of a wine, but also found in unhygienically bottled wines. In Spain it refers to a specific yeast that grows in Jerez and imparts a delicate, nutty quality to its wines. When Sherry is affected by this yeast, called *Saccharomyces fermentati*, it is called *fino*.

fortified A wine to which alcohol has been added to raise its alcoholic strength. These wines usually range from 15 to 21 percent alcohol.

free-run juice The juice that is released from the grape as it is being crushed, before the pulp and skins are pressed. This juice, generally less harsh than press wine, is used for the finest wines. Free-run accounts for about 60 percent of the juice available from the grape for fine wine. This juice is separated immediately from the skins for white wine but is combined with the skins and pulp for reds. It is drained off the solids prior to the pressing of the remaining grape material.

French oak The wood from the great oak forests of France, particularly from Nevers and Limousin, which is used to make aging barrels; this wood imparts a distinctive and mellow character to wine. The term *French oak* is also used to describe the actual flavor imparted to wine aged in French oak barrels.

generic wine A broadly used wine term signifying a wine type, as opposed to a more specific name, such as a grape variety or the actual region of production. Such names have frequently been employed on American wines using famous European place names such as Chablis, Burgundy, Rhine, and Champagne, or European wine types such as Claret and Sherry.

Goût de Terroir The specific taste characteristic imparted from the soil of a particular wine district.

Goût de Vieux The distinctive taste of an old wine.

Grand Cru   Literally "great growth." Refers to a classification of French wines considered to be superior in quality. Used in Bordeaux, Burgundy, and Alsace.

hybrids   New grape varieties genetically produced from two or more varieties. Usually defined as varieties created from different species, although the term is loosely used to include vines "crossed" within the same species.

hydrogen sulfide   A chemical compound that is a natural byproduct of fermentation. With proper handling it dissipates prior to the finishing of a wine, but in poorly handled wines, it remains (and you can tell because it imparts the smell of rotten eggs).

jug wines   Refers to inexpensive, everyday drinking wines, usually bottled in large bottles known as jug bottles. Most wines in this category are generics, but varietals also occasionally appear in jug bottles.

Late Harvest   Refers to a type of wine made from overripe grapes with a high sugar content. Generally, *Late Harvest* wines have been made from grapes deliberately left on the vine to achieve high sugars and concentrated flavors. White wine grapes are frequently affected by *Botrytis cinerea*, the noble mold, which further concentrates the grape and imparts its own unique honeyed character. Most *Late Harvest* wines are unctuously sweet, luscious in flavor, and are meant to be drunk with dessert or by themselves rather than with a meal.

lees   The sediment that results from clarifying a wine following fermentation in casks or tanks after separation from the skins and pulps. Usually consists of dead yeast cells and proteins. Wines are left on their lees to gain character and complexity; improper procedures can result in wines with unattractive flavors.

legs   The "tears," or streams of wine, that cling to the glass after a wine is swirled. It is usually a sign of a wine with body and quality and is caused by the differences in evaporation rates of alcohol and other liquids in the wine.

maderized Refers to a wine that has lost its freshness or has spoiled due to oxidation in the bottle, either from storage in an excessively warm area, or simply because of overage. Maderized wines tend to smell like the wines from Madeira, hence the term. They have an unattractive, sharp yet sweet, caramelized character. Maderized white wines darken in color to amber or brown.

Maître de Chai In France, refers to a winery's cellarmaster who is charged with tending the maturing casks of wine. Frequently he is also the winemaker. This position is the most important in a winery.

malolactic fermentation The secondary fermentation that occurs in some wines due to the action of certain bacteria, which transform the hard malic acid to softer lactic acid. It also imparts new subtle flavors, which, depending on the wine type, may or may not be wanted. It is usually undesirable in white wines, which require malic acid for freshness.

Méthode Champenoise The traditional method of making sparkling wine and the only one permitted in the French district of Champagne where sparkling wine was invented. It is the most labor-intensive and costly way to produce sparkling wine, but it imparts a character and refinement unattainable with other methods, particularly with regard to the quality of the bubbles produced.

middle body Refers to that part of the taste sensation experienced after the initial taste impact on the palate. It provides the core of the taste on which assessments are usually based. The first, or *entry*, taste and *finish* should both be in harmony with the middle body. A wine with a weak middle body generally gives the impression of being incomplete.

Mis en Bouteilles Sur Lie Literally, "put in bottles on its lees," this term refers to the practice of bottling a wine directly from the barrel, immediately after fermentation and without racking. The wine (almost always white) retains a fresh, lively quality, often with a slight *pétillance* due to the absorption of carbon dioxide (which had not completely dissipated when bottled) during fermentation. *Sur lie* wines often experience a malolactic fermentation in the bottle, which also contributes to the wine's *pétillance* (or "coming alive") in the bottle during the year after bottling.

must Refers to the unfermented grape juice produced by crushing the grapes. It is a loosely defined word that also refers to grape juice, crushed grapes, or the juice after pressing.

racking Refers to the traditional way of clarifying a wine: transferring it from one cask to another and leaving the precipitated solids behind.

residual sugar Refers to the unfermented sugar remaining in a wine. It is usually described in terms of the percentage by weight, and is detectable when it exceeds .75 percent. Above two percent, it tastes quite sweet.

robe Refers to the color of a wine in general, and, more specifically, to the wine's color when the glass is tipped at an angle.

sec Literally means "dry," and refers to a dry wine. Its use is not legally defined, and it frequently appears on wine labels of wines that are off-dry or even somewhat sweet.

sediment Refers to the deposit precipitated by a wine that has aged in the bottle.

sparkling Refers to a wine that, under pressure, has absorbed sufficient carbon dioxide to bubble, or "sparkle," when poured into a glass.

tannin   Refers to an astringent acid, derived from the skins, seeds, and wooden casks, which causes a puckering sensation in the mouth. *Tannin* is an essential preservative for quality wines. A moderate puckering sensation caused by the tannins adds to the pleasurable character of a red wine.

Tonneau   A Bordeaux measure of wine, equivalent to four barrels, or 100 cases of wine.

transfer process   Refers to a shortcut method of making bottle-fermented Champagne. In this process, the wine is filtered rather than riddled and disgorged. The transfer process produces wines that are sometimes indistinguishable from the more complicated method.

unfiltered   Refers to a wine that has been bottled without being clarified or stabilized by filtration. Such a wine might be clarified by fining, however. When bottled without any cellar treatment, such a wine is labeled as "Unfiltered and Unfined."

unfined   Refers to a wine that has not been fined as part of its cellar treatment. Also implies that the wine has not been filtered and has received a minimum of treatment.

varietal   Refers either to a wine named after a grape variety or to one made entirely from a single grape variety. Legally, such a wine need be made from only 75 percent of the named grape.

varietal character   Refers to the recognizable flavor and structure of a wine made from a particular variety of grape.

Vinifera, Vitis vinifera   Refers to those species of grape varieties known as "the wine bearers," which are responsible for all the finer wines of the world.

vinosity   Refers to the characteristic flavor of a wine as a result of fermented grape juice. It is distinct from any other flavors such as those of the unfermented grape, oak cask, or other flavor components.

viticultural area   A delimited region in which common geographic or climactic attributes contribute to the definable characteristic of a wine. Although it is called by different names in various countries, it is usually referred to as an Appellation of Origin. In the United States, such an appellation is called a "viticultural area" and is defined by geography alone, as opposed to requirements regulating the varieties of grapes grown, yield, or nature of wine produced.

volatile acid   Refers to the acid component of a wine, which can be detected in the aroma. In wine this is acetic acid, the acid of vinegar. It is always present in wine, usually in undetectable or low levels, adding to the complexity and appeal of a wine. When excessive it is an undesirable defect.

Index

Symbols

1855 Bordeaux Classification

A